# The Dressage Rider's Problem-Solver

# The
# DRESSAGE RIDER'S
# PROBLEM-SOLVER

*Barry Marshall*

The Crowood Press

First published in 1996 by
The Crowood Press Ltd
Ramsbury, Marlborough
Wiltshire SN8 2HR

Paperback edition 2001
© Barry Marshall 1996

**British Library Cataloguing-in-Publication Data**

A catalogue record for this book is available from the British Library.

ISBN 1 86126 410 0


**Picture credits**
Photographs by Anthony Reynolds LBIPP, LMPA
Line-drawings by Rona Knowles


**Acknowledgements**
Grateful thanks to Sandy Sargent and Ninja for
their help with the photographs in this book.


Typeset by Phoenix Typesetting, Ilkley, West Yorkshire

Printed and bound in Great Britain by The Bath Press, Bath

# Contents

# Introduction

This book is aimed at a wide range of riders, from those already competing in dressage to those just beginning. Anyone from Pony or Riding Club level through to Grand-Prix may be helped by referring to it.

The object is to provide solutions to problems encountered in riding dressage tests, which everyone – even the most experienced – has to face. Comments made by judges or trainers are often puzzling, and this book provides an interpretation of those comments.

In each chapter there is a description of what ought to be happening, and an analysis of the cause and effect of each problem, together with an explanation of what to do to make an improvement.

The reader will find that a certain amount of cross reference has been necessary as training problems are seldom isolated but are more generally related to other factors. For example where a horse is described as being 'on the forehand', there may also be a reference to the rider 'leaning forwards', which is under a separate heading.

Competitors should appreciate that although advice can be given as to making corrections, any problem can be completely put right only if sound systematic basic training is followed.

# CHAPTER 1

# The Rider

## Correct Position

The correct position in the saddle is a basic requirement for successful dressage riding. The rider's seat must be supple and flexible, upright and deep. The rider sitting correctly will be able to give correct and clear aids to the horse, without losing his balance or becoming 'untidy'. Probably the best way to acquire this position is on the lunge, without stirrups. In this way the rider is able to concentrate on his position without having to control the horse.

Development of the position on the lunge is advantageous if the lunge-horse is quiet and well mannered, and he is controlled by a knowledgable person. It is also a help if the animal has good paces that are comfortable to sit on. It can be very difficult to improve the seat if the horse gives a jolting ride.

The rider should sit in the centre of the saddle with equal weight on both seat bones. His back should be upright, but supple and flexible, enabling him to 'follow' the movement of the horse. The rider should look forward with a firm but not stiff neck. His thighs should be turned inwards from the hip and rest smoothly and firmly on the saddle. The foot should be parallel to the horse's side with the heel at the lowest point.

It should be possible to draw an imaginary straight line from the rider's shoulders, through his hips, to his heel. The rider's lower leg should be close to the horse's girth. His hands should be held just above the horse's withers, with elbows close to his sides, but not fixed or tight. Another straight line should be seen from the rider's elbow, through his wrist and hand, to the horse's mouth. The rider must learn to maintain this position at all gaits. A correctly fitted and balanced saddle is essential for the rider to be able to gain and maintain the desired position.

---

**Rules for Correct Position**

- Sit in the centre of the saddle.
- Relax the seat muscles and allow yourself to sit deep.
- Sit straight and sit up.
- Do not collapse your back.
- Keep the shoulders back without being tense or stiff.
- Hold your head up.
- Keep your legs close to the horse.
- Carry the hands just above the withers.
- Keep your elbows in and your toes up but be flexible in all the joints.

---

## Correct Use of the Aids

The aids – the hands, seat, back and legs of the rider – are the means by which we

*Correct position.*

convey our wishes to the horse. These aids should always be applied in a firm, concise and consistent way. Although the rider needs to be 'tough' at times and determined, he should never be 'rough'.

If the correct position in the saddle has been adopted, the rider's legs will be in close contact with the horse's sides where they will be able to give the aids. From a basic contact they should be able to squeeze the horse forwards. If there is a lack of response, firmer use by braced muscles in the calves of the legs may be more effective. Failing that, the schooling whip used behind the leg should bring about the desired result.

The rider should sit in the saddle with relaxed seat muscles to enable him to absorb the horse's movement. His back should be upright, having the ability to brace in order to strengthen the seat, but it must also be flexible, never rigid. Some riders have a tendency to 'shovel' the horse with the seat in a misguided effort to make him go forwards. This is not only unsightly but ineffective.

If held in the position already described, the rider's hands will be able to take and maintain a contact with the horse's mouth. This contact should be steady but elastic and should be 'conversational', not 'dead'. Effective action by the hands comes from a feel and ease contact: asking the horse for an answer and easing tension when the answer is given correctly. A loose rein or intermittent contact is like a disjointed conversation with someone who stammers or is at a loss to know what to say next!

The rider should be exact about what he is asking the horse to do and allow time for transmission to take place. The horse cannot reply in an instant: he needs time to understand messages sent to him by the

---

**Rules for Correct Use of the Aids**

- Think what you want to do and plan where you want to go.
- Warn the horse and give him adequate time to prepare.
- Give sympathetic but effective aids.
- Be consistent.
- Give the horse time to respond to your aids.
- If mistakes are made give him the benefit of the doubt.
- Teach the horse how you want him to answer.
- Be able to use a schooling whip.
- Use your voice to help the horse to learn.

---

aids and time to organize himself for a response.

## What each Aid Does

### Rider's Inside Hand

The rider's inside hand gives the direction to the horse and asks for the bend.

### Rider's Inside Leg

The inside leg should be placed on the girth, to create and maintain impulsion and to bend the horse. The horse should learn to answer a light pressure from the inside leg of the rider and should not need to be 'kicked' at every stride.

### Rider's Outside Hand

The outside hand controls the amount of bend created by the rider's inside hand and leg, and controls the speed and impulsion of the horse.

## Rider's Outside Leg

The outside leg is placed just behind the girth to control the hindquarters of the horse. On circles and turns, it prevents the hindquarters from swinging out and assists with the bend of the horse. Used with more pressure the horse should 'step away' from it as in half-pass.

## Rider's Seat and Back

The influence of the rider's seat and back aids will help to achieve the engagement of the horse's hindquarters and assist the horse to become properly balanced. The seat and back should be strong and secure but never stiff. The back should be upright, never collapsed at the waist or shoulders, and neither in front nor behind the vertical.

## Voice

Although the rider is not allowed to use his voice during a dressage test it is a most useful aid in the training of the horse, especially in the early days. If the young horse has been properly trained on the lunge before being ridden he will know the words of command, walk, trot, canter, etc., and it will be easier to teach the hand, leg and seat aids to him. The voice is also invaluable to correct the horse and also to praise him for good work done.

## Schooling Whip

The schooling whip is an 'artificial aid', used to back up the leg signals given by the rider. It should be used close to the rider's leg to help the horse to understand the aids. It should never be used to punish the horse.

## Spurs

The spur is an 'artificial aid', used to enable the rider to give finer aids, but it should never be used to punish the horse.

## Faults

### Against the Movement

A rider who is against the movement is not keeping his shoulders parallel with the horse's shoulders. This commonly occurs on a circle, when the rider pushes his inside shoulder forward rather than bringing the outside shoulder round to match the horse's shoulders; or in the lateral movements, the rider leans away from the flexion of the horse, or places more weight on the outside seat-bone rather than on the inside. The horse with the rider in opposition to the movement will not be able to show the correct flow and engagement required.

Think about where you are in relation to the horse's movement. If you imagine yourself to be part of the horse rather than a separate entity perched on top, you are more likely to match the horse's movement.

### Behind the Movement

This is a fault that is usually shown by the rider who leans back behind the vertical. From this position it is impossible to follow the movement of the horse with the seat and hands. This fault can also sometimes be seen at the start of the extended movements, when the horse goes away with more power than the rider expected and the rider gets left behind.

Work on the lunge without stirrups

*Hands too high.*

would be a great help to better the position and gain the feel of going 'with the horse'.

## Hands Not Level

Although it is acceptable at times for the rider's outside hand to be a little higher than the inside hand, most of the time the hands should be level. As with hands that are too wide apart, this fault is usually caused because the rider's legs are not effective enough. The rider is often seen to raise the inside hand to create the bend because the horse is not sufficiently responsive to the inside leg.

Assess your position and whether the legs are correctly placed so that they are able to be effective. Consider whether your leg aids are clear, and practise this.

## Hands Too High

Hands that are held too high will break the straight line from the rider's elbow through the wrist and hand to the horse's mouth. This often results in the hands' becoming unsteady, when the horse will show resistance and will often overbend as all the pressure from the bit will be on the corners of the mouth and not evenly distributed on the bars, tongue and lips.

Concentrate on riding with lower hands to gain a more 'elastic' contact with the horse's mouth. Consider whether you are feeling tense in your hands or elbows as this can cause the hands to rise.

## Hands Too Low

Riders often place the hands too low in an attempt to keep the horse's head down, but it usually has the opposite effect. The horse will fight against the extra pressure on the tongue and bars of the mouth and try to lift his head to relieve it.

Concentrate on your hands: practise carrying them and maintaining a firm but elastic contact with the horse's mouth.

## Hands Unsteady

Unsteady hands will cause the contact to be erratic and in turn the horse's head to be unsteady. Try to maintain a soft and elastic feel with the horse's mouth through the reins. Do not try to gain the steadiness of the hand by clamping the elbows to your sides as this creates static, rather than elastic, contact. Concentrate on developing a more secure seat, as most unsteady hands stem from an insecure seat and leg position.

## Hands Too Wide

Hands that are held too wide apart affect the rider's ability to follow the movement of the horse's head and neck correctly.

Usually the rider adopts this position because the leg aids are not sufficiently effective. So a more secure and effective leg position needs to be worked on. The bend and engagement of the horse must be produced and maintained from the rider's seat and legs, not the hands.

## Head Nodding

Some riders nod their heads in sitting trot in an effort to absorb the movement of the horse's back. This is not only incorrect but unsightly.

Relax the seat, sit deep and think about absorbing the movement through the seat and back, not just at the top of the spine. Work on the lunge without stirrups would be beneficial.

## Inconsistent Aids

Inconsistent signals will cause the horse to be confused and resentful and will not give rise to a smooth performance.

Make sure that you understand the correct aids for each movement, and practise them until you are giving them smoothly and consistently.

## Leaning Back

Many riders try to improve the influence of the seat by leaning back behind the vertical, but these thoughts are misguided. This position places too much weight on the horse's loins and makes the seat and legs of the rider ineffective. Leaning back is often accompanied by hands that are too high and lower legs that are too far forwards.

Firstly make sure that the saddle sits correctly on the horse and is not tipping back, forcing your seat too far back in the saddle. Concentrate on bringing your lower leg under your hip onto the girth, lowering the hands to the correct height. This will enable the seat, hands and legs to have the desired influence over the horse. Check the length of your reins: are you leaning back to take up slack that shouldn't be there? Adopting the leaning

*Upper body behind the vertical and lower leg forward.*

back position can also cause the rider to be 'behind the movement'.

## *Leaning Forwards*

Riders that lean forwards often carry the hands too low and the lower leg too far back. The whole art of dressage riding is to be able to engage the horse's hind-quarters, improve his balance and allow him to show freedom of the shoulders. This can be achieved only from a firm and influential seat, which is lost if the rider tips forward. Work on the lunge without stirrups is the best way to strengthen the seat and improve the position. Leaning forward is a fault often seen in tense riders. Practise relaxation in the seat. Check that the length of your reins is correct.

## *Leaning to Left or Right*

Most riders are stronger on one side than the other and on the weaker side are inclined to collapse the waist allowing the shoulder on that side to drop.

The rider will need help from the ground as this problem is rarely felt. Both stirrups must be of the same length and equal weight placed on both seat-bones, with the shoulders of the rider horizontal

*Rider leaning forwards, bringing the seat out of the saddle.*

to the horse's shoulders. If the rider remains 'one-sided', it will badly affect the horse's training and make it impossible for him to perform correctly.

## Legs Too Far Back

If the rider's lower leg is too far back the seat will be weakened and correct aids cannot be given. This problem is often accompanied by the rider's leaning forwards and carrying the hands too low.

Concentrate on keeping the lower leg on the girth, sitting upright and having the hands in the correct position. Relaxation exercises may help as leaning forwards

and the associated leg position may stem from tension and a fear of being 'left behind'.

## Legs Too Far Forwards

The rider whose legs are in front of the girth is not able to give the aids correctly, and the true influence of the seat will be lost.

To find the correct position for the leg, take your feet out of the stirrups, let the stirrups hang vertically and then place the ball of the foot on the stirrup iron. The stirrup leather should not be pushed backwards or forwards. Of course, this

*Lower leg too far forwards.*

*Lower leg too far back.*

will only work if the saddle is correctly balanced on the horse's back. By correcting this fault the rider will gain a stronger and more effective position. The problem may be caused by leaning back (*see* page 00).

## Looking Down

The rider who looks down usually accompanies this with rounded shoulders and hands that are carried too low.

This fault suggests a lack of confidence. As with all bad riding habits, help is usually required from somebody on the ground to correct the problem.

## Not Between Hand and Leg

At all times the rider should have control over the horse. A horse that is 'not between hand and leg' is not being sufficiently controlled by the rider's seat, hand and leg aids.

The rider needs to develop a stronger seat and use hand and leg aids that are able to influence the horse's way of going. Work on the lunge would be beneficial.

*Reins too loose.*

## Reins Too Long

If the reins are too long, the correct contact with the horse's mouth will not be maintained. If the horse chooses to come above or behind the bit the rider's hands will not be able to keep in contact with the horse's mouth and serious evasions may develop.

Horses are very clever at gradually taking the reins from the rider and this is usually because the rider's fingers are not closed on the reins. In an effort to control the horse the rider with reins that are too long will often round the wrists or take the

elbows back behind the body, both of which are bad faults.

## Reins Too Short

If the rider has the reins too short he will either have to lean forwards, straighten his arms too much or shorten the horse's neck and restrict the gaits in order to compensate. All of these are bad faults and must be corrected.

The rider must assume the correct position and take a firm but elastic contact with the horse's mouth.

*Reins too short.*

## Rough Aids

There is no excuse for the rider ever to use rough aids.

The rider must learn to control his emotions and train the horse to respond to the correct aids for the movement; these should be given concisely and consistently. This will take a lot of time, effort and patience but will bring its rewards at the end of the day. Frequently, a rider will blame the horse for not responding correctly, when the fault actually lies with the rider who is not making his wishes clear.

## Rounded Wrists

Most riders that round their wrists do so because their reins are too long. This is a bad habit as the correct feel and contact with the horse's mouth can not be found with the hands in this position.

Help from a person on the ground may be needed to break the rider of this habit.

## Spurs Incorrectly Used

The rider should wear spurs to be able to give 'finer' aids to the trained horse. They should not be used to punish the horse. A

*Spurs worn too low.*

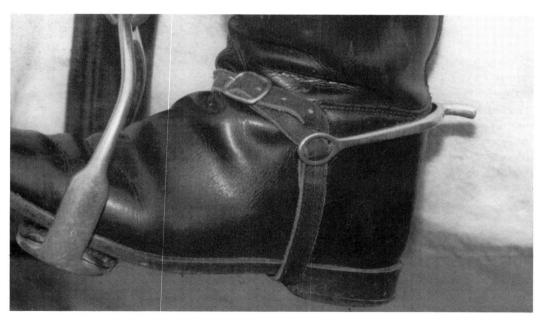

*This spur is at a better height but the arm should be level with the seam of the boot.*

rider should wear spurs only once he has achieved a secure seat and leg position, and understands precisely what the spurs are for.

## Spurs Incorrectly Worn

Spurs when worn should follow the horizontal seam of the rider's boot and should not be worn at 'half-mast', i.e. low at the heel and high at the front, or vice-versa, or low on the boot. Spurs should never be worn upside down with the shank pointing upwards.

## Stirrups Too Short

If the rider's stirrups are too short, the knee will sit too far forwards on the saddle, or even over the front of the saddle and the lower leg will be placed too far back, both of which will cause the rider's seat to be insecure and the aids to be applied incorrectly.

Remove your feet from the stirrups, let your leg hang loose from the hip, raise your toe a little and then adjust the stirrup to this length. Some riders ride with short stirrups because they are unable to remain deep in the saddle, especially at canter. The legs then creep upwards and the feet lose contact with the stirrup iron. If this is the case, work on the lunge without stirrups will help to develop a deeper, more secure seat.

## Stirrups Too Long

The rider with stirrup leathers that are too long will not be able to keep the heel as the lowest part of the foot and will therefore be insecure in the saddle.

A true and influential seat and leg position can only be maintained with a

*Stirrups too short.*

correct stirrup length. (*See* 'Stirrups Too Short' for adjusting length.)

## Toes Out

Riders sometimes ride with their toes pointing out instead of having them pointing to the front. By allowing this habit to develop the rider will not be able to give the aids correctly and, if spurs are worn, the effect on the horse can be quite cruel.

Work on the lunge without stirrups will strengthen the rider's seat and leg position.

*Stirrups too long.*

## Wrong Diagonal

The art of dressage is to make the horse equally supple on both sides and riding on the correct diagonal will help to achieve this goal. Most horses favour one diagonal and will try to put the rider onto it each time they trot.

The rider must persist with changing onto the correct one each time and as the horse becomes more supple the problem will lessen. For the less experienced rider, recognizing that the horse is on the wrong diagonal may be difficult. Help from the ground is necessary until the rider can 'feel' for himself.

## Conclusion

Riding problems can most easily be corrected on the lunge by riding without stirrups or reins or both. Most riders find faults creeping into their riding from time to time, but it is essential to conquer them quickly as it is hard to correct a fault once it establishes. Nearly everyone has a strong side and a weaker side which affects their position and the way the aids are given. Only by continually riding and determinedly practising can a weak side improve. Mental concentration and a strong resolve to improve are the answer.

---

**Rules for Good Riding**

- A good position can be achieved only when riding on a correctly fitted and balanced saddle.
- Regular check-ups are needed from a trained instructor to correct any bad habits that are creeping in to your position.
- Learn the aids and always use them precisely and consistently.
- When any resistance occurs from the horse, always check first that your own position is correct and that you are asking for the movement in the right way.
- Regular lunge lessons on a good horse from a qualified trainer is the best way to achieve a correct and secure position in the saddle.
- Although a good trainer is essential, only your own determination will make you a good rider.
- Aids given should be clear to the horse but not obvious to the person on the ground.
- Whips and spurs should be used only to 'fine tune' the horse, not to punish him.

---

# CHAPTER 2

# The Horse

The perfect horse has yet to be born and probably never will be, but when choosing a horse for competitive dressage at the higher levels the nearer he comes to perfection the easier the training will be. Nearly every horse would be capable of performing the movements of the Grand Prix test if correctly trained but if they have a conformational fault or are 'limited' in their gaits they will never be able to show the brilliance and outline required of the really top horse.

## Breed of Horse

Many different breeds go in and out of fashion as dressage horses but at the end

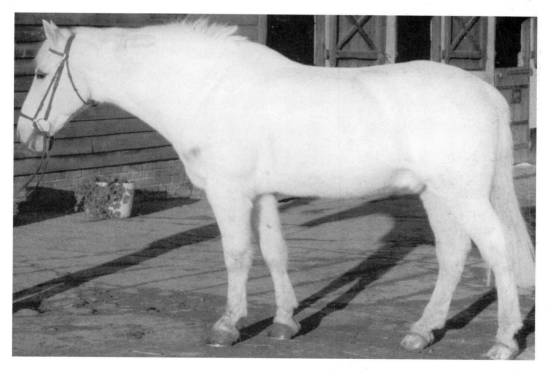

*This type of horse would be unsuitable for dressage.*

of the day the conformation, temperament and the gaits are what matter, not the breeding. The Thoroughbred can be a very attractive animal and many have been trained to the highest levels, but for many riders they are too sharp and fizzy and often lack the ability to bend the hind leg sufficiently for the most advanced movements. The cold-blooded and draught breeds generally lack the athletic ability required of a top horse. The Three quarter-bred is probably the most suitable of all: the high percentage of Thoroughbred blood gives him height, boldness, good looks and impulsion, and the other quarter – be it draught, Arabian, Gelderlander, Trakhener, Welsh Cob, etc., – gives a steadiness to the temperament and a rounder action. The most important things are that:

1. The gaits are true, free and expressive.
2. The conformation is suitable for the job required.
3. The temperament is right for that particular rider, and
4. The horse is the right size.

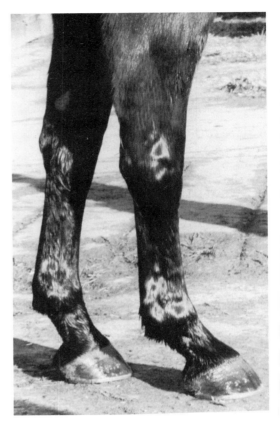

*Back at the knee.*

## Faults

### *Back at the Knee*

A horse that is back at the knee places more stress on the tendons and may not remain sound, so such a horse is therefore not to be recommended as a potential dressage horse.

### *Blemishes*

Blemishes on the horse – such as scars, old injuries, etc. – should not stop him from

becoming a successful dressage horse, as long as they do not interfere with the horse's joints, mouth or saddle area.

### *Broken Neck*

A neck that bends too far down rather than at the poll. This may be caused by the neck being very long.

### *Canter Faults*

As with all the gaits the horse should have a correct, free and expressive canter.

Although the gaits will improve with training I would not recommend starting with a horse that has a basic fault to the canter, such as a four-beat rhythm.

## Dipped Back

A horse with a dipped back is not ideal for dressage as he may find it too difficult to assume a round shape and to engage correctly from behind.

## Dishing

Dishing does not preclude a horse from dressage; in fact, many top horses have carried this fault. Having said that I would not choose a horse that dished as aesthetically it is never pleasing to the eye.

---

**Fitting the Rider**
It is most important that horse and rider 'fit' each other. A very tall rider on a small horse will never look right to the eye and a very tall horse may be difficult for the small rider to train.

---

## Forging

Forging is when the toe of the hind shoe catches on the heel of the forefoot and makes a clicking noise. It may only happen occasionally or, in some cases, quite a lot. It occurs in trot and is caused by lack of balance. As the horse learns to engage his hindquarters correctly to raise the forehand, the fault should cease, so it is not a problem that would prevent an otherwise good horse from succeeding at dressage.

## Grinding Teeth

Horses that grind their teeth usually do so through fear or temper. Marks will be lost in competition if the judge feels the grinding is affecting the performance. If the problem is caused by fear or tension the rider needs to reassure the horse and possibly ask himself whether he is asking too much of the horse for his age or stage of training. Teeth grinding that is combined with a swishing tail usually denotes temper and the rider needs to work to gain better acceptance of the hand and leg aids.

## High Behind

A horse that is built higher at the croup than at the withers will never look as engaged as the horse that is level front and back. The more advanced movements will be difficult for him to perform as he will have to lower his croup a long way to lift the forehand sufficiently. I would not recommend this type of horse for dressage.

## Long Back/Long-Coupled

A horse with a long back will find it diffi-cult to take his weight on to his hindquarters in order to show the true collection and engagement required of an advanced dressage horse. If the long-backed horse has a correspondingly long front, the picture will still be pleasing to the eye, but if the long back is accompa-nied by a short neck the outline will never look good enough to gain high marks. One advantage of the long back is that the horse usually finds the lateral movements easier to perform than the very short-coupled horse does as he is more able to show the bend round the rider's leg.

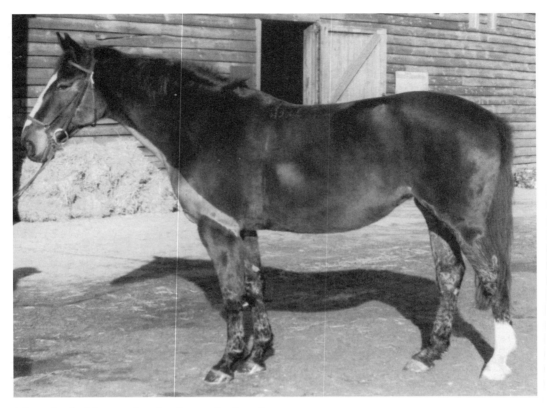

*A long-backed horse who also has a short neck.*

## Long Neck

Fully and correctly trained, the horse with a long neck will present a most elegant picture, but may give the rider problems on the way. It is very easy for the long willowy neck to overbend and to bend too far back from the poll (broken neck). Great care must be taken throughout the training to develop the muscles correctly so that the neck becomes elegant and not swan like.

## Lop Ears

There is nothing wrong with training a

lop-eared horse for dressage, as physically it does not affect the performance; but if the ears are really low or out to the side the ultimate picture will not be as pleasing as that created by a horse with normal ears.

## Low-Set-On Neck

A neck that is set on low, instead of rising out of the top of the withers can be very difficult to train into the correct shape. If the rider attempts artificially to raise the head and neck, a large muscle will develop under the neck and be not only most unattractive but incorrect. I would not

*The length and shape of this neck would hinder training.*

consider a horse with this conformation fault for future advanced work.

## Low-Set-On Tail

Although a low-set-on tail is not particularly attractive, it should not hinder the horse in any way from becoming a successful dressage horse.

## Over at the Knee

A horse that is over at the knee usually has no problems with soundness because of it and should not be discounted as a potential dressage horse.

## Poor Gaits

The more expressive the gaits, the more attractive and high-mark earning will be the finished article. The most important criterion is that the gaits are correct and true. I would rather have a horse with three moderate, but correct, gaits than a horse with an impressive trot but a poor walk and canter.

## Short Back/Short-Coupled

A horse that is very short-coupled has an advantage over the long horse in that he finds it easier to engage the hindquarters

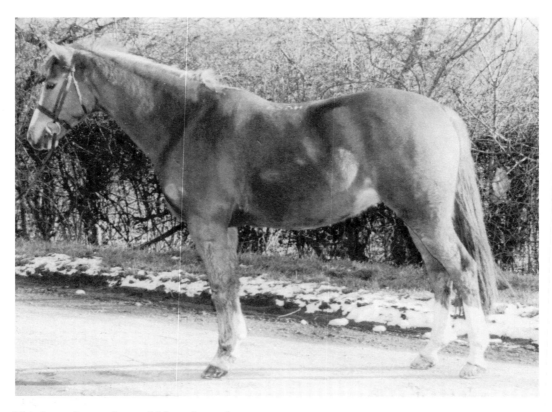

*This horse has rather a thick underneck.*

under the body sufficiently to lift the fore-hand. However, an over-short back does create some problems in that it often makes bending sufficiently for the lateral movements difficult, and it can also be difficult to sit on as the 'engine' tends to be under the saddle.

## Short Neck

A horse with a short neck will never appear as elegant as the horse with a good long neck, and if accompanied by a long back the picture will never please the eye of the judge. Great care must be taken in the training to keep the neck as long as possible and not artificially to shorten it further. Many horses with an over-short neck are also rather thick through the jowl, which can cause problems to the horse when he is required, as the training advances, to arch his neck.

## Straight Hind Legs

A horse with a straight hind leg is not to be recommended as a dressage horse because he will find it too difficult to engage the hindquarters correctly, which requires the horse to bend all the joints of the hindleg.

## Stringhalt

Stringhalt is a condition which causes the horse to 'snatch' his hindlegs up, sometimes in walk, sometimes in walk and trot. Some riders have misguidedly thought that this would aid a dressage horse, confusing the snatching of the hocks with engagement. When a horse engages correctly he steps well under his body with the hindlegs, with all the joints well bent. A horse with stringhalt steps up and down not under. Such a horse with this condition is not suitable for dressage.

## Sway Back

*See* 'High Behind'.

## Temperament Faults

The horse's temperament is very important if you wish to compete successfully. Very few horses are born with a bad temperament but many are started badly and many are just being ridden by the wrong people. What is a bad temperament for one rider may be good for another. If you have an 'electric' seat, choose a horse that is not highly strung. If you have a weakness in your seat choose a horse that is naturally forward going. Nervous riders should have a horse they feel safe on. A horse that is either excessively fizzy or sluggish may be difficult to train for dressage, and will require considerable time and patience.

## Trot

It is of the utmost importance that the horse is sound and that the gait is true. A horse that naturally trots in balance, engaging from behind and showing

---

### Rules for Choosing the Right Horse

- The horse must be the right size for the rider.
- Choose a temperament that suits yours.
- Only experienced riders should take on young or unbroken horses.
- If possible let your trainer guide you with the purchase.
- It is better to have three moderate gaits than one outstanding one and two poor ones.
- When viewing a horse, bear in mind that the musculature can be changed with correct training but the basic structure cannot.
- Soundness is of paramount importance.

---

freedom of the shoulder will be so much easier to train than the horse with limited ability. A natural aptitude for 'lengthening' is a great asset.

## Unsoundness

Soundness is of the utmost importance. A dressage horse needs three totally sound gaits. Too often horses that are unsound are seen in the arena: to my mind these horses should not be ridden. Veterinary advice should be sought if any unlevelness is shown in the gaits. Dressage places a great strain on the horse especially in the hindquarters so soundness at the start is imperative.

## Walk

The walk should be free, regular and true, showing a good, clear four-beat rhythm. A natural ability to extend the walk is a great asset. A limited walk will lose many marks in competition.

## *Weak Hocks*

A horse with weak hocks or poor hindquarters will find it very difficult to perform the advanced movements and, if asked to do so, lameness might result. As the horse progresses through the levels he is required to take more and more weight onto his hindquarters, and he will find this almost impossible if there is an inbuilt weakness.

# CHAPTER 3

# Saddlery

There is no doubt that a correctly fitted and balanced saddle will enable the rider to sit in an elegant and effective position and give the horse maximum comfort. The bridle must also be fitted with the horse's comfort in mind and to enable the correct action of the bit used.

## The Saddle

The saddle should fit the horse *and* the rider and be placed in the correct position on the horse's back. A dressage saddle is a must for the serious competitor if the desired position is to be achieved.

Although it is not impossible to sit in the correct dressage position in a general-purpose saddle, it is not easy. A general-purpose saddle, having a rounded flap, will allow the rider's knee and lower leg to slip forwards unless the stirrups are shorter than would be desired of a dressage rider.

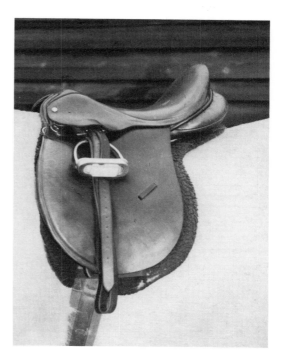

*A correctly fitted saddle that should sit the rider in the right place.*

## Tips Back

A saddle that tips back will not only be uncomfortable for the horse but will put the rider into the wrong position and make it very difficult for him to remain upright in the saddle and keep the leg in the desired position. Viewed from the side, the seat of the saddle should be horizontal rather than sloping forward or backward.

## Tips Forward

A saddle that tips forward – that is, one that is higher at the back than at the front – will encourage the rider to tip forwards, thus making the rider's seat less effective. (*See* 'Tips Back' for guidance on checking fit.)

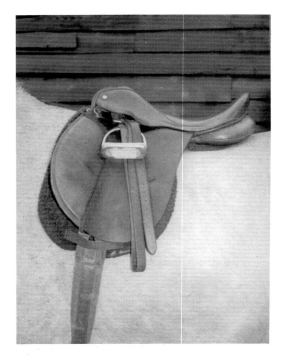

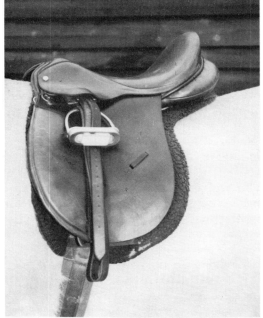

*This saddle would throw the rider backwards.*

*This saddle sits up off the horse's back, so it does not fit correctly.*

## Too Big

If the saddle is too big for the horse it will sit too far back on the loins and cause him much discomfort. If the saddle is too big for the rider, it will be difficult for him to sit still in the correct position and to avoid sliding from front to back and vice-versa.

## Too Far Back

It is difficult to explain in words the correct place for the saddle to sit on the horse but it must not be so far forwards that it sits on the shoulder and restricts the movement of the horse's fore-hand, nor should it sit too far back where excess weight would be placed on the loins;

this latter position will cause discomfort and encourage the horse to hollow his back.

## Too Far Forwards

The saddle that is either placed too far forwards, or one that slips into this position after the rider is mounted, will place too much weight on the horse's fore-hand and make correct balance difficult. If the horse is such a shape that any saddle will slip forwards, a fore-girth may be used. This looks rather like an anti-cast roller and is put on before the saddle. The front part of the saddle is placed up against it and is thus prevented from slipping forwards.

## Too Small

If the saddle is too small for the rider he will find it very difficult to sit in it and maintain the correct position. The flat part of the seat must be large enough for the rider, who would otherwise be pushed onto the pommel by the rise at the cantle.

# Bridles

The bridle should fit the horse properly: the bit must be of the right size and be correctly adjusted, and the leatherwork should be of the right weight for the horse. Nothing looks worse than a horse with a small head overloaded with wide leather straps, or a horse with a large head wearing very narrow leather.

## Bit-Guards

Bit-guards are not permitted to be worn in competitive dressage and should not be necessary if the bit is fitted correctly and has no sharp edges.

## Cavesson Noseband

A cavesson noseband may be used with a snaffle bit and should be correctly fitted so as not to interfere with the bit. With a double bridle, this type of noseband is compulsory.

## Curb-Chain

A curb-chain is used with the curb bit of a double bridle and must be correctly fitted to give the horse maximum comfort and to allow the action of the bit to be used in the way designed. A rubber or leather cover may be used on the chain.

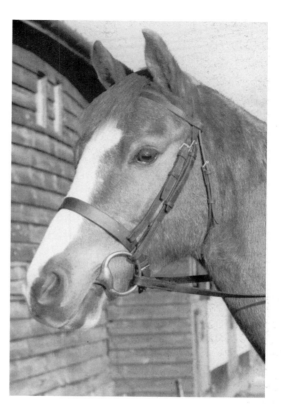

*A correctly fitted snaffle bridle with cavesson noseband.*

*Too Loose*

Curb-chains that are too loose are too often seen in the dressage arena. If they are adjusted in this way the curb bit will have the wrong action, causing excess poll pressure, and if the bit has a port, this will push forwards into the roof of the horse's mouth and cause him great discomfort.

*Too Tight*

If the curb-chain is too tight, the horse will be in great discomfort and will show many resistances to try to alleviate the pressure on his mouth. The curb-chain should be adjusted so that its action comes into play only when the rider uses the curb rein. A chain that is too tight will be in play all the time.

## Drop Noseband

A drop noseband may be worn with a snaffle bridle and should be correctly fitted. It must not be so high as to lift the bit in the horse's mouth, nor so low that it affects the horse's breathing. It is a mistake to try to gain the horse's acceptance of the bridle by over tightening the drop noseband as the horse will only be

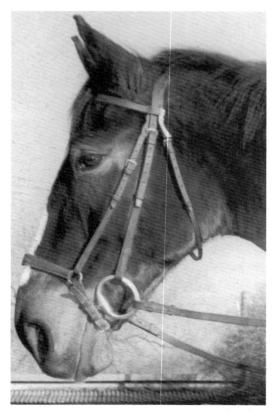

*A snaffle bridle with drop noseband. The throatlash is too loose.*

uncomfortable and show even more resistance.

## Double Bits

There are many different types of bridoon and curb bit available. Some bridoons have one joint, some two. There are loose ring, egg-butt and hanging-cheek bridoons. Curb bits may be half-moon, have a tongue groove or a port, have a fixed or a sliding cheek. You must first of all find out which bits are permitted by the F.E.I. or your National Federation then find the bit that suits your particular horse. Both bits must always be correctly adjusted in the horse's mouth.

### Too Close Together

The two bits in the horse's mouth must be adjusted so that they do not sit on top of each other. The bridoon bit should be fitted as a normal snaffle and the curb lower in the mouth. The bridoon must not be too long for the horse's mouth, or the joint will hang down onto the curb bit.

## Flash Noseband

A flash noseband may be worn with a snaffle bridle, but not with a double bridle, and should be correctly adjusted. The higher (cavesson) part of the noseband should be fitted as an ordinary cavesson noseband. When the lower part of the noseband is fastened it should not be so tight as to pull the cavesson down at the front. Horses that dislike a drop noseband often take more kindly to the flash as there is less pressure on the nose.

## Fly-Fringes

It is permissible for the horse to wear a

*A correctly fitted double bridle.*

*Bridle with a flash noseband. The browband is rather low.*

fly-fringe while being ridden in at a competition, but it must not be worn during the test.

## Reins

It is most important that the width of the reins that you use are the right width for you. Some people like a wide rein, others a narrow one; neither is incorrect but they must feel right to you. When using a double bridle the top rein (bridoon) should be thicker than the curb rein.

## Snaffle Bits

The many different types of snaffle bit all have a slightly different action on the horse's tongue, lips and bars of the mouth. There are snaffles with one joint, others with two. There are loose-ring and egg-butt types, and some with cheeks. They are made of metal, rubber or other synthetic materials. You must first find out which bits are permitted in competition by your National Federation and, of those, find the bit that is most suitable for your particular horse's mouth. The bit must be of the correct size and fitted properly.

### Too High

If the snaffle bit is adjusted too high in the horse's mouth it will cause him much discomfort and lead to resistance. The bit should just wrinkle the lips slightly when placed in the mouth, not give the horse a permanent grin!

### Too Large

Many people misguidedly think that they are being kind to the horse by fitting a bit that is too long, but especially with a jointed snaffle bit the opposite is the case. The joint will hang too low in the horse's mouth causing it to touch the front teeth, at which point its nut-cracker action is increased, causing much pain to the horse. There is also a danger that the horse will learn to get his tongue over the bit, a habit that will then be hard to break.

### Too Low

If the bit is placed too low in the horse's mouth there is a great danger that he will learn to put his tongue over the bit. Once this fault has become established it can be very difficult to eradicate. There may also

*This picture shows a snaffle bit that is too large and low in the horse's mouth.*

be a problem if the bit is so low that it hits the horse's teeth. This will cause him much pain and will lead to serious resistance. If the bit is the correct size, but still too low in the mouth, the cheekpieces should be adjusted.

*Too Small*
It is of the utmost importance that the bit

you choose to ride the horse in is of the correct size for him. If the bit is too small it will cause his mouth to become sore, especially his lips, and lead to many forms of resistance.

## *Tongue Layers*

If a horse has become confirmed in the habit of putting his tongue over the bit it may be necessary to use a 'tongue layer', to help break the habit. This should be correctly fitted and, if you are not sure how, expert help should be sought. The wearing of tongue layers is not permitted in dressage competition.

---

**Rules for Good Saddlery**

- The tack used must first of all fit and be comfortable for the horse.
- A dressage saddle is a must for the serious competitor.
- The saddle must be well balanced, tipping the rider neither forward nor back.
- No two horses' mouths are the same, and expert advice should be sought to find the right bit for your horse.
- Tack should be cleaned and checked regularly for comfort and safety.
- The curb-chain should always be correctly and comfortably fitted.

---

# CHAPTER 4

# The Gaits

## The Walk

The walk is a marching gait in which the footfalls of the horse's feet follow one another in 'four time', well marked and maintained in all work at the walk. The purity of the four-beat rhythm must be preserved at all costs; it should never be sacrificed while teaching the horse new movements.

## *Medium Walk*

The medium walk is a free, regular and unconstrained walk of moderate extension. The horse, remaining on the bit, walks energetically but calmly with even and determined steps; the hind feet touch the ground in front of the footprints of the forefeet. The rider maintains a light, soft and steady contact with the horse's mouth.

The rider should feel that the horse is relaxed, taking the biggest stride of which he is capable without any tension or loss of rhythm.

*Rules for Medium Walk*

- Follow the horse's natural movement – do not 'shovel'.
- Be purposeful.
- Do not interfere with the length of the horse's natural stride but, rather, encourage him to keep it.

- If you are not sure if the horse is 'overtracking', ask someone on the ground to help you.
- Do not restrict natural movement of the horse's head and neck.
- Keep contact with legs and hands.
- If the horse hurries, restrain him quietly.
- Make sure his hindlegs are following his forelegs.
- Encourage concentration in the horse with the 'feel and ease' pressure you apply with the aids.
- Feel for a definite rhythm of steps.

## *Free Walk on a Long Rein*

The free walk on a long rein is a pace of relaxation in which the horse is allowed complete freedom to lower and stretch out his head and neck, while the rider maintains a very light contact with the horse's mouth. The horse remains active, straight, in a true four-beat rhythm, and overtracks.

*Rules for Free Walk on a Long Rein*

- Do not prevent the horse from stretching in the first instance by being too slow to give him the rein.
- Give the rein gradually and encourage him to stretch.
- If he breaks rhythm correct him as quickly as possible.

*Horse accepting the bridle in walk.*

- Keep a light contact.
- Look at the marker towards which you are heading, and ride straight.
- Do not have a loose rein.

## Free Walk on a Loose Rein

Like the free walk on a long rein, the free walk on a loose rein is a pace of relaxation in which the horse is allowed complete freedom to lower and stretch out his head and neck, but the rider releases all contact with his mouth. The horse remains straight and well forward on a long stride.

Although the rider should release the contact with the mouth, the legs must stay on the horse to keep him straight and forward going.

## Extended Walk

At the extended walk the horse covers as

*Walk on a long rein. The horse's nose should be in front of the vertical.*

much ground as possible, without haste and without losing the regularity of the steps. The hind feet touch the ground clearly in front of the footprints of the forefeet. The rider allows the horse to stretch out his head and neck without, however, losing contact with the mouth.

## Collected Walk

The horse remains on the bit, moves resolutely forward, with the neck raised and arched. The head approaches the vertical position, the light contact with the mouth being maintained. The hind legs are engaged with good hock action. The gait should remain marching and vigorous, the feet being placed in regular sequence. Each step covers less ground and is higher than at the medium walk, because all the joints bend more markedly, showing clear self-carriage. In order not to become hurried or irregular, the collected walk is shorter than the medium walk, although showing greater activity.

*Rules for Collected Walk*

- Increase contact with the legs first before collecting with the hands.
- Use a half-halt to bring the horse together.
- Never restrict forward movement.
- Never 'collect' by drawing the horse's front in with your hands.
- Expect to feel submission to the bit.
- Do not let the horse become crooked.

## *Walk Transitions*

Transitions within the walk (collected – extended – collected), and transitions from the other gaits to and from walk should be direct, straight and without resistance. The horse must accept the collecting aids when he is required to go from extension to collection and he must immediately lengthen his steps and his frame when asked to go from collection to extension. The acceptance of the hand, seat and leg aids are imperative if good transitions are to be achieved.

*Rules for a Good Walk*

- Practise the walk each day; do not just use it as a rest period.
- At all times, consider the 'purity' of the gait as your number one priority.
- In medium, extended and long rein walks, although you must have a contact with the horse's mouth do not restrict the natural movement of the horse's head and neck.

- Always keep your leg aids in place on the horse in walk, even if he is threatening to jog.
- Do not practise collected walk for too long a period.
- Practise taking up the reins and then releasing them again, so that the horse does not always think that he is going to trot or canter after walk.

### Faults Commonly Occurring in Walk

*Medium Walk*:
- Hollow Back
- Mouth Open
- Neck Short
- Steps Short
- Tongue Out
- Rhythm Not Always True

*Free Walk on Long Rein*:
- Head too High
- Jogging
- Not Overtracking
- Reins Too Loose

*Free Walk, Loose Rein*:
- Not Straight
- Not Stretching Down

*Extended Walk*:
- Lacking Freedom of the Shoulder
- Lacking Purpose
- Loss of True Rhythm
- Not Extended

*Collected Walk*:
- Lacking Collection
- Lateral
- Nose Behind Vertical

## The Trot

The trot is a gait of 'two time', on alternate diagonal legs (near fore and off hind leg and vice-versa), separated by a moment of suspension. The trot should always show free, active and regular steps, and should be moved into without hesitation.

## *Working Trot*

This is a gait between the collected and the medium trot, in which a horse not yet trained and ready for collected movements shows himself to be correctly balanced and on the bit, going forwards with elastic steps and good hock action. The term 'good

hock action' does not mean that collection is a required quality of a working trot: it only underlines the importance of impulsion originating from the activity of the hindquarters.

It is important that the rider learns to feel whether his horse is moving correctly at the working trot as this is the gait at which most of the foundation work will be practised. To assess the trot from the saddle the rider needs to ask himself several questions: Does the horse feel 'in balance' (not heavy on the forehand)? Is he able to make turns and changes of direction without altering the gait? Is he accepting the hand and leg aids without resistance? Has he enough impulsion to

*Rider's upper body behind the vertical in an ineffective position.*

*A good active trot; the neck is a little short.*

jump a small fence from this trot? If the answer to these questions is Yes, the gait is probably correct. If the answer to any of the questions is No, the rider must look for the cause.

Viewed from the ground the horse in working trot should appear 'active', but not 'hurried'. He should be in a rounded outline showing no resistance to the rider's aids. The rider with the aids in place should not have to work too hard to maintain the gait, which would mean that the horse is not sufficiently attentive to the aids.

The working trot may be ridden sitting or rising. The more novice rider is best advised to work mainly at the rising trot so that he does not put undue pressure on the horse's back or disturb the rhythm of the movement.

*Rules for Working Trot*

- Make sure it is balanced.
- It must be going forwards actively.
- There should be a regular and clear rhythm.
- The horse should be on the bit and be accepting his rider's aids.
- Do not sit to the working trot unless your seat is sufficiently secure.

## Lengthened Trot

The lengthened trot is a gait between the working and the medium trot. It is the first step towards medium and extended gaits. The horse, while remaining in balance and on the bit, should lengthen the steps and the frame but not hurry or show irregularity.

Before asking the horse for lengthened strides, the rider must be sure that the working trot is straight, in balance and with sufficient impulsion. The lengthening may be practised on a straight line or on a circle. The rider will 'close' both legs on the horse's sides to create more impulsion and allow the horse to lengthen his outline a little, being sure not to let him go on to the forehand. If the horse answers the rider's aids and gives extra length to the steps he should be returned to the working trot after a few strides and rewarded. If the strides just become hurried, the rider will need to rebalance the horse and begin the exercise again.

The lengthening may be ridden in sitting or rising trot but in the early days is usually best practised at the rising trot to encourage the horse to round his back.

*Rules for Lengthened Trot*

- Do not start this until the horse's working trot is well established.
- Never try to lengthen the trot if the horse is on his forehand.
- The horse must be straight.
- The steps must be in exact rhythm.
- Build up to it gradually.
- Make transitions at either end clear, but do not rush them.

## Collected Trot

At the collected trot the horse remains on the bit and moves forwards with his neck raised and arched. The hocks, being well engaged, maintain an energetic impulsion, thus enabling the shoulders to move with greater ease in any direction. The horse's steps are shorter than in the other trots, but he is lighter and more mobile.

The collected trot is very often difficult for the more novice rider to assess. Although the steps are shorter than in the other trots they must not be restricted. The neck is raised and arched but this comes about by extra activity from the hindquarters, not from the rider's attempting to lift the neck with the reins.

The collected trot is always ridden 'sitting'.

*Rules for Collected Trot*

- Do not slow the gait or restrict the steps.
- Engage the hindquarters actively.
- Bring the horse to collection by using half-halts.
- Keep the horse straight.
- Overcome resistance with sensitivity, not force.

## Medium Trot

The medium trot is a pace between the working and the extended trot, but more round than the latter. The horse goes forward with free and moderately extended steps and an obvious impulsion from the hindquarters. The rider allows the horse, while remaining on the bit, to carry his head a little more in front of the vertical than at the collected and working trot, and allows him at the same time to lower his head and neck slightly, but without going onto the forehand. The steps should be as even as possible and the whole movement balanced and unconstrained.

The horse should be asked to perform the medium trot only when he is able to produce well-balanced, lengthened strides. Once he is able to maintain the lengthened strides for longer periods of time, more impulsion and energy may be created to produce the medium trot. This the rider will do by placing both legs more firmly on the girth.

The medium trot is always ridden in sitting trot in competition but during the early stages of learning the movement is usually best practised rising so that there is no danger of the rider's interrupting the rhythm and balance.

*Rules for Medium Trot*

- The horse must be balanced and impulsive.
- He should be able to lengthen and collect.
- The transitions must be ridden properly.
- Be secure in your sitting trot.
- Build up the distance you want to go gradually.
- The same rules apply for extended trot.

## Extended Trot

At the extended trot the horse covers as much ground as possible. Maintaining the same cadence, he lengthens his steps to the utmost as a result of great impulsion from the hindquarters. While remaining on the bit, and without leaning on it, the horse is allowed to lengthen his frame and gain ground. The forefeet should touch the ground on the spot towards which they were pointing when suspended. The movement of the fore- and hindlegs should be similar (more or less parallel), in the forward movement of the extension. The whole movement should be well balanced and the transition to collected trot should be smoothly executed by taking more weight onto the hindquarters.

The rider will develop the extended trot from the medium trot. Once the medium trot can be maintained for a full side or diagonal line of the arena, the horse may be asked to produce greater energy and activity from the hindquarters and thus a longer stride. The rider must create the energy by using both legs on the girth and be keeping a light but steady contact with the horse's mouth.

In the arena, the extended trot is always shown with the rider sitting, but at home it may be practised rising.

## Trot Transitions

The horse should make clear, direct and straight transitions within trot (collected to extended, extended to collected, and so on), and to and from other gaits. If problems are evident in the transitions it usually means that the gait was incorrectly prepared, for example the head was up at walk when canter was asked for. Rather than working at the transition alone the rider needs to concentrate on getting a better walk; the horse must be sufficiently engaged in the walk to be able to make the strike-off, he must be attentive to the rider's aids and prepared properly for the transition. Good transitions can only be shown if the horse accepts the rider's hand, seat and leg aids.

To make a correct transition from walk to trot the rider must first ensure that the walk is active, straight and that the horse is 'on the bit'. Both legs are then applied to the girth, the hands should lighten but the contact must not be lost. The horse should move smoothly into trot without delay. If this does not happen the rider should re-establish the walk and try again. Only in this way will the horse learn what is required of him.

To make a transition from trot to walk the rider must first ensure that the horse is balanced and listening to his aids. He should sit deep in the saddle, close his legs onto the girth and apply more pressure to the rein. At first the horse will be allowed to come gradually to walk but as the training progresses the transition will become clearer and more direct. As soon as the horse comes to walk the rider should relax the pressure of the hands so as not to restrict the forward movement of the strides.

*Rules for Good Trot*

- Change your diagonal at each change of direction.
- Sitting trot should be practised only for short periods on a young horse or if the rider's position is insecure.
- Sitting trot is best practised on the lunge with an experienced teacher.
- Do not ask the horse to lengthen his trot unless the working trot is well established in rhythm and straightness.
- Any irregularities in the trot should be investigated by a veterinary surgeon before trying to find other causes.

**Faults Commonly Occurring in Trot**

*Working Trot*
- Above the Bit
- Hurried Steps
- Lacking Activity
- Lacking Impulsion
- Not Forwards Enough
- On the Forehand
- Too Deep

*Lengthened Trot:*
- Irregular Steps
- Running

*Collected Trot:*
- Head Too High
- Lacking Collection
- Neck Short
- Not Straight

*Medium Trot:*
- Lost Balance
- Not from Behind
- Running at Start

*Extended Trot:*
- Against the Hand
- Not Ridden Out to Marker
- Wide Behind

## The Canter

The canter is a gait of 'three time'. At canter to the right, for instance, the foot-falls follow one another as follows: left hind, left diagonal (simultaneously left fore and right hind), right fore, followed by a moment of suspension with all four feet in the air before the next stride begins. The canter should always have light cadence and regular strides, and it should be moved into without hesitation or resistance.

The canter should feel springy and light, not heavy or sprawling; the horse must not lean on the hands. To achieve good balance in canter the rider will find the half-halt the most effective method.

When watching a horse canter the moment of suspension between each three-beat stride should be clear. This can happen only if the horse has sufficient impulsion.

To achieve a correct strike-off to canter the rider should: sit in the saddle; control the pace with the outside rein, taking a flexion to the leg he wishes the horse to lead with; place his inside leg on the girth to control the bend and to send the horse forwards; and position his outside leg just behind the girth to control the hindquarters, maintain bend and warn the horse which leg to canter on; the inside leg should then be used to start the canter.

## *Working Canter*

This is the gait between the collected and medium canter, in which a horse not yet trained and ready for collected movements shows himself to be properly balanced and on the bit, going forwards with even, light, cadenced strides and good hock action. The expression 'good

*The working canter.*

hock action' does not mean that collection is required of working canter; it only underlines the importance of impulsion originating from the activity of the hindquarters.

*Rules for Working Canter*

- The horse must be obedient to the strike-off aids.
- Good balance is achieved by using half-halts.
- The rider must concentrate on gaining a definite rhythm.
- The gait must always be three-beat.
- The hindquarters should always come 'under' the horse.
- Bend should always be towards the leading leg.

## Lengthened Canter

This is the gait between the working and medium canter. The horse lengthens his stride and his frame but remains straight, in balance, on the bit, and in a true three-beat rhythm.

*Rules for Lengthened Canter*

- Do not ask for lengthening if the horse is leaning on the hands.
- Make sure he is straight and does not put his quarters in.
- Do not allow the stride to change rhythm from working to lengthening.
- Control the transitions adequately.

## Collected Canter

During collected canter the horse remains on the bit and moves forwards with his neck raised and arched. The collected canter is marked by the lightness of the forehand and the engagement of the hindquarters, that is, it is characterized by supple, free and mobile shoulders and very active quarters. The horse's strides are shorter than at the other canters, but he is lighter and more mobile. The purity of the three-beat rhythm must be maintained at all times.

*Rules for Collected Canter*

- Collect by degrees using half-halts.
- Make sure that the hindquarters do not swing.
- Deal with resistance firmly but sympathetically.
- When learning, do not expect too much at one time.
- If the horse is anxious, ride forwards.
- Practise equally on both reins.

## Medium Canter

This is a gait between the working and the extended canter. The horse goes forward with free, balanced and moderately extended strides and an obvious impulsion from the hindquarters. While remaining on the bit, the horse is allowed to carry his head a little more in front of the vertical line than at the collected and working canter, and at the same time is allowed to lower his head and neck slightly. The strides should be long and even and the movement balanced and unconstrained. The three-beat rhythm must be retained throughout the medium canter.

*Rules for Medium Canter*

- Build up to medium canter from good collection.

*The rider has her heels up, weakening the effect of the leg, and her rein tension is making the horse overbend.*

- Ride clear transitions.
- Do not allow the horse to lean on your hands.
- Make sure the rhythm is held.
- Be certain that the hindquarters are not 'coming in'.
- Practise equally on both reins.
- Do not allow the horse to take control away from you.
- The rules for extensions are the same but it is important to show a distinct difference between the two.

## *Extended Canter*

In the extended canter the horse covers as much ground as possible. Maintaining the same rhythm, he lengthens his strides to the utmost, without losing any of his calmness, lightness and straightness, which results from the great impulsion from his hindquarters. While remaining on the bit, and without leaning on it, the horse is allowed to lower and extend his head and neck, the tip of his nose pointing more or less forward. The horse should go smoothly and directly to and from the extended canter at the rider's command .

## Canter Transitions

Canter transitions within the gait (collected to extended to collected), or from one gait to another (walk to canter to walk, for example), must be smooth, straight, direct, and free from resistance or loss of balance. Obviously the degree of directness of the transition will depend on the level of training of the horse: the higher the level of training, the more direct the transition. Riders must beware not to confuse direct with abrupt. In a direct transition the horse will go from one gait to the other smoothly and without any intermittent steps; an abrupt transition will have a moment of hesitation, caused by the rider's stopping the 'flow' of the transition.

*Rules for Good Canter*

- Practise the canter equally on both sides.
- Be supple in your body and arms so that you can go with the horse and not restrict the natural movment of the head and neck.
- At all times be aware of the straightness of the horse: a slight flexion to the leading leg is required but the hind feet must follow the front feet.
- Never sacrifice the purity of the gait in an attempt to achieve collection.
- Give the aids for the strike-off concisely and consistenly.
- Never allow the horse to take control from you when teaching medium and extended canter.
- Collection must be obtained from a greater degree of activity and 'stepping under' of the hind legs, not by use of the rein alone.

### Faults Commonly Occurring in Canter

*Working Canter*:
- Canter Flat
- Croup High
- Disunited
- Lacking Bend
- Lacking Jump
- Wrong Lead

*Lengthened Canter*:
- Not Straight
- Hurried

*Collected Canter*:
- Grinding Teeth
- Lacking Collection
- Lost Three-Beat Rhythm
- Stiff
- Tilting Head

*Medium Canter*:
- Bucking
- Late to Start
- No Clear Transitions
- Not Enough Difference
- On the Forehand
- Swishing the Tail

*Extended Canter*:
- Against the Hand
- Hollowing
- Not Ridden Out to Marker
- Resistance at Marker

# Faults

## Above The Bit

*In all gaits*
A horse that is working above the bit will be developing his muscles in all the wrong

*Head too high. Rider tipping forwards and no contact.*

places. His head will be too high, allowing the muscles under the neck to develop. His back will be hollow, preventing the hindlegs from working correctly under the body. He will be unbalanced. Viewed from the ground the horse will have a hollow, rather than rounded, topline. Horses may work in an 'above the bit' outline for several reasons: the rider may be too rough with the hands, causing pain in the horse's mouth; the rider may be too heavy in the saddle causing the horse to be uncomfortable in his back; or he may simply have not been taught to answer the aids correctly when first ridden.

Using the hand, leg and seat aids, you must encourage the horse into a rounder outline, making him accept the bit. If the problem is only slight, you will be able to ride the horse's head lower by riding more positively forwards into an 'asking' hand. If the problem is acute, you will probably need to go back to walk and teach the horse better acceptance of hand and leg aids before progressing to trot.

## Against the Hand

### In all gaits

Horses that have not been trained correctly in the early stages will find it

*This photograph shows several faults. The horse is on his forehand and therefore lacks balance. He also has his mouth open.*

difficult to maintain their balance in the extended trot gaits and may try to 'lean' against the rider's hands for support in the movement. Even though the horse is required to lengthen and lower his neck in the extended canter he must remain on the bit. If the horse goes against the rider's hand in the extension he has taken control away from the rider.

If the horse is against the hand in extended trot, you must go back a stage or two and work at the lengthening and medium trots until the horse is able to balance without leaning.

If the problem occurs at extended canter, you will need to work on the lengthening of the canter on a circle where it will be easier to keep the horse's hindquarters engaged and to keep him up into the bridle. As soon as he tries to go against the hand the rider should half-halt him and then send him forwards again with strong seat and leg aids. Repeat the exercise until he will lengthen without resistance.

This problem is very common and crops up in many situations. If any resistance occurs the rider should check on his aids and his manner of giving them. An aid given suddenly, lack of preparation or consideration for the horse are the common causes.

## Bucking

*In medium canter*

Bucking can be an act of exuberance or a resistance to the rider's leg aids. Either way it must be corrected before it becomes a bad habit.

The first thing to do is to keep the horse's head up as he can only really buck if he drops his head down. At the same time he must be driven forwards with the legs. Many riders make the mistake of using less rather than more leg in this situation but this is just what the horse wants you to do. The horse must not be allowed to blackmail the rider into not using the leg aids correctly. It would probably be best to practise the medium canter on a circle until you have complete control over the canter, then work on a straight line may be resumed.

## Canter Flat

*In canter*

The three-beat rhythm of the canter strides are separated by a moment of suspension. It is this suspension that makes the canter gait expressive and enables the horse to gain ground. In a flat canter the moment of suspension has been almost lost.

Activate the horse's hindquarters more, bringing the horse's inside hindleg further under his body so that he is more able to spring off the ground.

## Croup High

*In canter*

If the horse is croup high it means that he has not lowered his hindquarters sufficiently or placed his hind feet far enough under his body. In effect he is carrying more weight on the front legs than on the back legs.

Go back a stage and teach the horse to answer the hand, seat and leg aids correctly. Work on a circle is easier than on the straight line as it is easier to engage the horse's inside hind leg on a curve. Make sure that the canter is forwards and active and then, by a series of half-halts, ask the horse to engage more from behind. Progress will probably be slow as the horse will have to build up strength in his hindquarters in order to be able to take more weight on them.

## Disunited

*In canter*

Young horses will often 'disunite' the canter to avoid taking the weight onto their inside hindleg.

As soon as you feel the change of leg behind, bring the horse back to trot and start the canter again. You will probably need to gain more control with your 'outside' aids to stop the hindquarters from swinging out, as this is what the horse usually does when he disunites the canter.

## Grinding Teeth

*In all gaits*

Horses that grind their teeth may do so for one of two reasons: anxiety or anger.

The first is easier to deal with. You need perhaps to progress more slowly and make sure that the horse understands and is physically able to perform what is being asked of him. Once he has gained confidence the grinding will normally stop. A horse that grinds his teeth in anger will usually swish his tail at the same time. If this is the cause of the problem you will need to rethink your horse's whole training programme. Take the horse back to a lower level and teach him to answer the aids correctly and submissively. If this form of resistance is not curbed right away it can be very difficult to stop at a later stage.

## Head too High

### In free walk

This fault occurs when the rider lengthens the reins. Rather than lowering and stretching out his head and neck, while remaining in a rounded outline, the horse raises his head, and will probably hollow his back and shorten his steps at the same time.

You will need to re-take the contact and with stronger leg aids ride the horse more forwards into a rounder outline. Once the head lowers, allow the horse a longer rein as long as he seeks down not up. If after a few steps the horse raises his head, the exercise should be repeated until the horse's head and neck will remain low.

If the horse has been working properly, he should want to stretch and lower his head when the rein is given. If this does not happen, and the aids do not seem to be working, try an additional feel on the mouth accompanied by a slight, alternate action of the hands. This should be subtle and soft and the rein offered immediately afterwards. The process may be repeated until the horse does stretch.

### In collected gaits

If the horse works with his head too high in the collected gaits the rider should return to the working gait and produce a more secure roundness. The collection should only be asked for a few steps at a time and any loss of roundness should be countered by riding the horse forwards to, for example, working trot, before asking for collection again. True collection can only be achieved if the horse is round in outline and working correctly through from behind.

## Hollow Back

### In all gaits

This means that the topline of the horse from the nose to the tail has become concave instead of convex. A hollow back indicates that the horse has come off the bit and is not able to step correctly under the body with the hindlegs. In consequence the steps will be too short and often hurried.

You must teach the horse to accept a correct contact with the reins, lower his head and neck, and round his back. Use your legs to encourage the horse to go more forwards. Hollowing can take some time to correct if the horse is allowed to go in this way for too long, as the muscles gradually become shortened along his topline, making it very difficult to correct the problem. Patience and perseverance are needed, but it is essential that the problem is addressed quickly because, if the horse is allowed to continue in this way, the quality of the gait will gradually be impaired.

You must also consider whether you are causing the hollowness. Too strong a contact and stiff arms may be the culprits. Although contact with the horse's mouth

*Rider pulling back on the reins, causing the horse to hollow.*

must be maintained through the reins, you must ensure that your arm is supple and follows the natural movement of the horse's head.

## Hollowing

*In extended canter*

If the horse hollows as he goes forward into extended canter, you will need to go back a stage in the horse's training and practise the lengthening of the stride. This is best done on the circle where it is easier to keep the horse engaged. If the horse starts to hollow, drive the horse forwards with strong seat and leg aids in to a 'resisting' hand until the horse relaxes his jaw and rounds his outline. Although we want the horse to be round and lengthen his frame at the extended canter we do not want him to go on the forehand, so keep the horse well engaged from behind. Once you are able to produce and keep the roundness at the lengthening on the circle, you can proceed to medium and then to extended canter on a straight line.

*Rider attempting collection, but the rein tension is causing the horse to hollow.*

## Hurried Steps

*In lengthened canter*

The strides of the horse must be controlled by the rider: he must not be allowed to rush forwards.

Huried steps may be caused by tension, in which case you need to reassure the horse by talking to him or stroking his neck. They may also come about if the horse is not accepting the rider's leg and seat aids or is unbalanced. As with all problems the riders must try to assess the reason and then take appropriate action.

Control can most easily be gained by riding on a circle, half-halting the horse each time he tries to rush forwards. Keep your legs in place on the horse's sides and do not feel that you must take them away to stop the rushing as this only causes further loss of control.

Many riders make the mistake of hurrying rather than lengthening the strides in lengthened canter. Again work should being on a circle. A good, active working canter should be established, and then you should increase pressure from the inside leg on the girth to ask the horse to take a longer stride. If the horse increases speed instead of lengthening, half-halt and keep repeating the exercise until longer steps are achieved.

## Irregular Steps

*In lengthened trot*
This fault often occurs in lengthened trot, and may happen for several reasons. The horse may lose his balance and fall onto the forehand; stiffness in one shoulder, hind leg or the back will also prevent regular steps; or the rider may get 'left behind', unbalancing the horse.

To address the problem, first ensure that the working trot is rhythmic, active and in balance and that the horse is straight. The lengthening should then be practised only a few steps at a time until the horse is able to balance for longer periods. Ensure that you go 'with the horse' and keep him straight.

## Jogging

*In walk*
The horse breaks the walk rhythm and assumes that of the trot for one or more steps.

Too often, the rider feels blackmailed into taking his legs away from the horse's sides. This is the opposite to what you should do: the horse must learn to stay on the aids at all times and must not threaten the rider.

## Lacking Activity

*In working trot*
In working trot the horse should show a marked degree of activity and impulsion

from his hindquarters. He must be encouraged to do this in the early stages of training, although the steps must not be hurried or made irregular.

Some horses are naturally active, others, especially those with straight hind legs or with a lazy disposition tend to be inactive.

The rider must assess whether the lack of activity is due to laziness on the part of the horse or to weakness. In the former case, use the leg and seat aids to make him go more energetically forwards. If the horse is not very responsive to the leg aids, it may be necessary to use the schooling whip to help create the activity.

If weakness is responsible for the problem, the horse must be allowed more time to become stronger behind before he is asked to work with more activity.

## Lacking Bend

*In canter*
In canter, the horse should always be bent to the leading leg, even in counter-canter. A canter that is lacking bend means that the rider has allowed the horse to come off the aids.

Work on a circle must be practised, the horse being made to listen to the rider's leg, seat and hand aids, especially the inside leg, which is the one that the horse should be bending round. The amount of bend required will be dictated by the size of the circle or turn: the smaller the circle the more bend required, as the horse should be uniformly bent to follow the line of the circle.

## Lacking Collection

*In walk*
A lack of collection means that the rider

has not shortened and activated the medium walk to the point of collection.

The horse must be asked to be more active from behind and arch his neck more. At the same time, take care to preserve the true rhythm of the walk; and do not hurry the steps. Also be alert to the horse's feeling tension or anxiety, which can be recognized by stiffness in the horse's back, grinding teeth or swishing tail.

*In trot*
To show true collection the horse needs to be able to maintain engagement and energetic impulsion. If your horse fails to do this, you must first ask yourself whether your horse is ready to collect his trot and, if so, for how long can you expect him to maintain it. In the early days of collecion only a few steps should be asked for before riding forwards into a brisk working trot. Gradually the horse may be asked to maintain the collection for longer periods of time. The collection is produced and maintained through your seat and legs, which create the impulsion, and with half-halts to control the balance and impulsion. The lateral movements should be ridden to engage further the hind legs of the horse, to strengthen the hindquarters and to enhance the bending of the hindleg joints.

*In canter*
If the horse lacks collection in canter he is not sufficiently engaging his hind-quarters.

This is most easily rectified by working on a circle, and the collection achieved from the working canter by means of a series of half-halts. These exercises should not be repeated for too long at a time until the horse's hindquarters are strong enough to maintain the collection for longer and longer. When trying for more collection you must beware of using only the hand aids to achieve it as this only produces a more restricted, not a more collected, canter.

## Lacking Freedom of the Shoulder

*In walk*
This fault most frequently occurs in the extended walk, when the horse appears to be walking into the ground rather than over it; he is on the forehand and not stepping through and under enough with the hind legs.

This can often be improved by use of the lateral movements, encouraging the horse to step further under with his hind feet. Encourage more activity, but not speed as this makes the steps even shorter.

## Lacking Impulsion

*In all gaits*
Some horses have a natural desire to go forwards and others are rather lazy by nature. It is the job of the rider to create impulsion and at the same time control it. There is no point in having a lot of impulsion if it cannot be controlled and used.

Energy gained from the seat and legs should encourage the horse to take longer steps, placing his hindlegs well under his body. Impulsion incorrectly used can put the horse on the forehand or just make him hurry the gait. If he is reluctant to answer the leg aids the schooling whip may be used to back up these aids. (The whip should only ever be used to 'back up' the leg aids, never to pu 'sh the horse.)

## Lacking Jump

*In canter*

This fault occurs in the canter, and is very similar to a flat canter: the moment of suspension of the stride is almost lost and the horse is in danger of showing a four-beat rhythm.

The rider must work on activating and engaging the hindquarters. The best exercise for this is to work on a large circle and practise going from working to medium canter and back to working again. If half-halted correctly, the energy gained from the medium canter should 'lift' the working canter.

## Lacking Purpose

*In walk*

The horse lacks activity and purpose, for example, showing a walk on a long rein rather than an extended walk.

Clearer leg aids are required to activate the horse and make his hind legs more active and purposeful, without hurrying or disturbing the rhythm.

## Lateral

*In walk*

This fault occurs mainly in collected and medium walk. In an attempt to collect the rider allows the four-beat rhythm to be lost and the walk to become a 'pacing' movement.

Great care should be taken at all times to preserve the true gaits. Ride energetically forward and attempt to collect the walk only a few steps at a time; then ride actively forward again. The collecting is best attempted on a circle, as the rhythm is more likely to remain true. The horse must be kept in a round outline and not be allowed to raise the head too high or to hollow his back.

## Late to Start

*In canter*

If the medium or extended canter is late to start, it is either because the rider has not given clear enough aids to the horse, or because the horse has not responded quickly enough.

If the former is the case, you must be more positive with the aids and ride the movement a little more boldly. In the latter case, the horse must be made to respect the aids more: it may be necessary to use the schooling whip with the leg aids to get the desired result.

## Loss of Balance

*In trot*

Balance is most often lost when, in an effort to make the steps longer in medium or extended trot, the rider allows the horse to fall onto his forehand.

Return to producing the lengthened trot, making sure that the horse maintains a correct balance. The medium trot should only be attempted once the lengthening can be ridden in balance.

## Loss of Three-Beat Rhythm

*In canter*

Often the true three-beat rhythm of the canter is lost during collection because the rider has misunderstood what true collection is. Riders often try to achieve the collection by slowing the stride by restricting the horse with the hand; this causes stiffness through the horse's back and destroys the moment of suspension in the stride. Ride forwards, preferably on a circle, into an active working canter and work to engage and activate the hindquarters. Once this is achieved, use a series of half-halts to ask for a little collection. Any loss of jump to the stride must be corrected by actively riding forwards and then repeating the exercise until collection can be achieved without loss of the three-beat rhythm.

## Loss of True Rhythm

*In walk*

In an attempt to ride the horse more forwards into an extended walk, the rider upsets the four-beat rhythm of the gait. Once established this can be a very difficult fault to eradicate.

Slow the rhythm and regain the correct footfalls. Lateral work in walk can often help this problem, as will walking on circles rather than straight lines. This will encourage suppleness and obedience to the aids, which in turn helps to establish a good rhythm.

## Rhythm Not Always True

*In walk*

The preserving of the true rhythm of the walk is of the utmost importance, and the rider must be careful never to disturb this rhythm when trying for longer or shorter steps. *See* 'Loss of True Rhythm' for suggested approach to this problem.

## Mouth Open

*In all gaits*

An open mouth shows that the horse is not accepting the contact of the rider's hands.

First check that the horse has no physical problems with teeth, lips or tongue. Having eliminated these possible causes, use a drop or flash noseband and work on exercises that will teach the horse to accept the hand. Make sure that it is not your hand that is causing the opening of the mouth: for example, in walk the rider's hands and arms should follow the slight movement of the horse's head and neck, not restrict it.

## Neck Short

*In walk*

This problem is caused by the rider restricting the natural movement of the horse's neck at the medium, collected or extended walk. It occurs most often in collection when the rider uses his hands more than his legs. The horse's nose is drawn in and his neck pulled back, instead of his hindquarters being engaged and being brought to a state of collection via the half-halt.

Use a softer hand and arm and stronger leg aids to encourage the horse to step more energetically forwards, allowing the neck to lengthen and round.

*In trot*

If the horse is producing a short neck at the collected trot, it will be because the rider is trying to produce the collection by restricting with the hands rather than by engaging the horse from behind.

Work the horse energetically forwards in a working trot, bringing the horse well up into the bridle. The gait should be collected by the correct use of the half-halt. (*See* 'Lacking Collection'.) If at any time the horse shortens his neck, ride him forwards again into the working trot. Be careful at all times not to restrict the neck or the gaits with the hands.

*Neck short; croup high.*

## Nose Behind Vertical

*In walk*
This problem may be caused by the rider's having too strong a contact or a stiff arm, making the horse feel restricted.

If the horse brings his nose behind the vertical in, for example, the collected walk, you should ride more actively forwards into a medium walk and begin the collecting exercise again. Use your legs on the girth to keep the horse up to the bit, and at the first signs of the nose coming back ride him forwards again. Once the required amount of collection has been achieved, soften (but do not give away) the contact.

## No Clear Transitions

*In canter*
This fault occurs most frequently in medium and extended canter. To show clear transitions the horse must be trained to be responsive, obedient and submissive to the rider's aids. The degree

*Rider shortening the neck for collection, rather than engaging the hindquarters.*

of directness of the transition depends on the level of the test being performed. A horse at elementary standard may go through working canter to achieve collection, but at advanced levels the horse must make a direct transition to collection, or from collection medium canter.

## Not Enough Difference

*In canter*

If not enough difference is shown between the collected and medium canters, it indicates either that the rider has not asked the horse to lengthen the strides enough, or that the horse has not responded to the rider's aid. Many riders show a lack of boldness in the arena and show little differences when they are asked for.

Make sure that there is enough engage-

*Rider looking down and horse overbent.*

ment and impulsion in the gaits to produce the length of stride required for a medium canter. No movement will come off well unless the preparation is correct. The collected canter should be active, impulsive and well engaged so that when the medium canter is required you can send the horse immediately forwards onto a longer stride. No control must be lost during the medium canter and you must be able to make the transition to the collected canter smoothly, calmly, straight and without resistance.

## Not Extended

*In extended gaits*
This means that the horse is not taking a sufficiently long and energetic stride in the extended gaits, possibly because the rider is frightened to push the horse in case he breaks the stride.

You must be bolder and encourage the horse to go more forwards with a longer stride, but take care not to hurry or upset the rhythm of the gait.

## Not Forwards Enough

*In trot*

This comment may be made about any one of the trot gaits. It is very important that the horse learns to show an active impulsion from the hindquarters in the working trot, as this trot is the basis of all later trot work. Without energy, impulsion, activity and a desire to move forwards, collection in the later stages is very difficult to achieve.

You must produce the impulsion required without letting the horse 'hurry' or become unbalanced. A horse that naturally goes forwards will be easier to train than the horse that is reluctant or lazy. However, ensure that the lack of forward movement is not of his own making: are the hands restricting the forward movement of the horse or are you merely not asking him to go forwards enough?

## Not from Behind

*In trot*

Some horses show an exaggerated front leg action that is not equalled by the hind legs. The fault occurs in medium or extended trot. The front legs appear to take a longer stride than the hind legs; in reality, they may step out a long way but they return to the ground behind the point of the extended part of the toe, rather than in front of it.

Return to the working and lengthened trot to make sure that the horse is correctly engaged. He must be made to lengthen the stride without hollowing or stiffening his back. Attempting the medium trot on a circle instead of in a straight line may help to keep the hind legs correctly engaged.

## Not Overtracking

*In walk*

With this fault, which occurs in the walk gaits (except the collected walk), the horse does not walk energetically forwards with an active hind leg and a free shoulder, and the hind feet come to the ground behind the print left by the fore-feet.

Taking care to preserve the four-beat rhythm of the walk, send the horse forward from stronger and more effective use of the legs. Also, ensure that you are not restricting the length of the walk stride by not allowing the horse the natural movement of his head and neck.

## Not Ridden Out to Marker

*In medium and extended gaits*

Many riders start the medium or extended gaits with a great flourish, but then let the impulsion and length of stride 'die away' before the end of the movement. In consequence, the horse has insufficient extension to show a clear transition to collection at the required marker.

The horse's strength and impulsion must be gradually built up over the course of his training so that he is able to maintain the extension for the transition to collection. it is a good idea to practise the extension on a circle, or – if ridden on the long side of the arena – to make the transition at A or C so that the horse does not anticipate stopping at the quarter marker every time. The rider should learn to 'use' the impulsion and energy of the extension to improve the collected gait; if the extension has died away this is not possible.

## Not Straight

### In all gaits

This fault occurs at a number of gaits, but it is generally caused by loss of activity and forward movement. It can also be caused by stiffness to one side, the horse being continually bent to left or right. Lack of straightness may also be caused by the rider using more pressure with one hand or leg.

### In walk and trot

To activate the horse, and encourage him to take longer, more positive steps, use your legs on the girth, but be careful not to hurry the steps. Stiffness can be improved by working on lateral movements. The horse must at all times be worked equally on both reins so that the muscles on each side develop at the same rate.

In the collected gaits, horses will often try to avoid 'collecting' by going crooked, thus avoiding placing the inside hind leg under the body. As soon as the lack of straightness is noticed, ride the horse more energetically forwards and begin the collecting exercises again.

You must be aware that at any gait, any crookedness on your part may be the cause of the loss of straightness in the horse. If you are not able to feel whether you are sitting straight, seek help from somebody on the ground.

### In canter

In canter, it is of the utmost importance that the horse remains straight: although he should be bent towards the leading leg his hind feet must follow the forefeet. Deviation of the hindquarters, in or out from that line, is the result of the rider's loss of control. The rider must take care

to make the horse responsive to the aids and to ensure that they are consistently used. Work on a circle to start with, making sure that the horse remains between the hand and leg; once this has been achieved you can return to work on the straight line. In order to control straightness in canter, a shoulder-fore position may be taken. This is not a full shoulder-in position; rather it is a matter of bringing the shoulders slightly away from the wall so that the hindquarters have room in the track and are therefore able to follow the forehand.

## Not Stretching Down

### In free walk

If the horse has been worked correctly in a round outline and with an active hind leg, he should want to lower his head and neck when allowed a loose rein.

If this does not happen you must question your training of the horse. Has he been working actively enough? Was he in a round enough outline? Is he accepting the aids? Work at the medium walk, encouraging the rounded outline and forwardness of the gait, before attempting walk on a loose rein. Once the horse starts to seek the rein downwards, you should be able to lose the contact but keep the horse forward, round and straight with the seat and leg aids.

## On the Forehand

### In canter

To work correctly the horse needs to be in balance. When he is on the forehand he is not stepping far enough under his body with his hind legs and is therefore unable to lighten his shoulders. Each time he puts his front feet to the ground, too much of his

*On the forehand and falling in.*

body weight is placed on them. Both from the ground and from the saddle he will appear to be moving in a 'downhill' direction rather than 'uphill'.

Use your back, seat and leg aids to encourage more activity in the horse's hindquarters, and combine these with the half-halt to raise the forehand. Do not try artificially to raise the horse's head and neck alone as this will just cause the horse to be hollow. Working the horse on a circle will encourage him to step further under himself with his inside hindleg and thus

bring him off the forehand. Bear in mind that this is not a problem that can be cured overnight; the horse needs to be gradually 'strengthened' behind so that he is then able to carry more of his weight on his hindquarters.

If the horse is on the forehand in the medium canter, you will need to go back a stage and gain the correct balance in the collected and working canter. Once the horse has learnt to balance correctly in the working canter, progress to lengthened strides. When this can be achieved without the horse going on the forehand, work on the medium canter can be resumed. Practise just a few steps at a time and, if any loss of balance occurs, half-halt and then ask again. Gradually you should be able to produce the medium strides for the whole length of the arena without loss of balance.

## Reins Too Loose

*In walk on a long rein*
This fault occurs when the rider confuses the long-rein walk with the walk on a loose rein.

You must regain contact with the horse's mouth, but be sure not to restrict or disturb the lengthening of the horse's head and neck. (*See* 'Free Walk on a Long Rein'.)

## Resistance at Markers

*In extended/medium transitions*
Resistance can be seen at the start or the finish of the extended or medium canter. Resistance at the start is usually caused by the rider's leg aids, when more pressure is applied to achieve the extension. Resistance to 'collecting' at the end of the extension is usually down to the rider's hands.

Either problem should be solved by going back a stage and working the horse on a circle, lengthening and shortening the canter. Apply the leg aids firmly and consistently to produce the lengthening until the horse accepts without resistance. To produce a better transition to collection, practise the half-halt.

## Running

*In lengthened and extended trot*
If you are lucky your horse will naturally lengthen his steps when you ask him to go more forwards; if you are not, he will probably just quicken his steps and 'run'. This habit must be checked right at the start so that it does not become an established problem.

You must first ask yourself whether the horse is ready to lengthen. Is he able to maintain his balance in an active working trot, for example? Is he inclined to go on the forehand or rush at the working gait? If the answer is Yes, these problems must be sorted out before the lengthening is attempted again. Some horses will find it easier to lengthen on a straight line and some find it easier on a circle; only trial and error will determine which is appropriate for you. Riding forwards from the leg aids must be countered with the half-halt so that the stride lengthens rather than quickens. Attempt only a few steps at a time and keep re-establishing a good working gait.

## Running at Start

*In medium and extended trot*
If the horse 'runs' at the start of the medium or extended trot it means that the collected gait was not sufficiently engaged: he feels obliged to run in order to build up the energy and impulsion required for medium or extended strides.

More impulsion and engagement need to be built into the collected trot, for example, so that the horse is able to make the transition directly to the medium trot. Try going from shoulder-in to medium trot as this will help to engage the hindlegs of the horse more.

## Steps Short

*In all gaits*
To resolve this problem the horse needs to go more energetically forwards and cover more ground with each step; but beware of quickening the rhythm of the gait as this may have the opposite effect and shorten the steps even more. Short steps are often accompanied by a short neck so the rider must be careful not to restrict with the reins.

## Stiff

*In collected gaits*
To be able to show true collection, the horse needs to be supple through his neck and back. Any stiffness shown when producing the collected gaits should tell the rider that the work at the working gait has not been correctly achieved.

If the stiffness shows up in all the horse's work, you must go back to the lower levels and, using the school figures and lateral movements, make the horse more supple. If the problem is showing only in the collected canter, for example, it indicates that you are probably trying to achieve the collection by too much use of the reins and not enough of the seat and legs.

## Swishing the Tail

*In all gaits*
If the horse swishes his tail he is either not accepting the rider's leg aids correctly or the rider is not keeping his legs secure on the horse's sides.

Usually as the horse accepts the aids better his resentment of the use of the leg fades. Some horses show their annoyance at being made to work more than others, but whatever happens they must eventually do what they are told. Consistent, clear aids and perseverance should help to overcome this problem. Be sympathetic: do not forget to praise the horse for better work so that his attitude becomes co-operative rather than angry.

## Tilting Head

*In collected gaits*
A horse that tilts his head is evading the pressure of the bit on one side of his mouth. This fault is often accompanied by lack of sufficient use of the hind leg on that same side.

Work the horse at the working gaits to gain better acceptance of the bit and engagement of the inside hind leg before progressing to the collected gait again.

## Tongue Out

*In all gaits*
As with an open mouth, this fault indicates that the horse is evading the true contact of the reins.

First check to make sure that there are no sharp teeth or cuts in the horse's mouth. If all proves to be well, a flash or drop noseband should be used and the horse encouraged to accept the bit by correct use of the hands, seat and legs. This problem must be corrected as it is often followed by the horse's getting his tongue over the bit, thereby completely evading the rider's contact.

Sometimes it is necessary to use flexions to overcome this problem. A flexion is a yield by one side of the horse's mouth and then the other, resulting in a small flexion of his head where it joins his neck. This helps to soften muscles that have become set and also encourages the horse gently to chew and 'give' to the bit. This helps him to feel comfortable and makes him concentrate better. Any flexions should be taken gradually and with great care. Any swinging of the head from side to side must be avoided.

Make sure that the contact you have with the horse's mouth is not causing the problem. A contact via the reins to the horse's mouth must be maintained, but the arms must be supple so that the natural movement of the horse's head and neck is not restricted.

## Too Deep

*In all gaits*
Some trainers like to work the horse 'deep', that is to say with the neck and back very rounded, often with the head quite low. Although this can be very beneficial it can also be very dangerous if used by the inexperienced rider because, once the horse has learnt to put his head and neck in this position, only strong use of the back, seat and leg aids will bring him back to the correct outline.

Although working the horse deep means that his head is lowered, he should not be allowed to go on the forehand or to drop back behind the bit, even if the nose is behind the vertical. Ensure that he is always able to bring the head and neck back to the correct position. The horse must never be ridden in this outline in competition as it is not a required element of a dressage test.

## Wide Behind

*In extended and medium trot*
Most horses that go wide behind in the extended or medium trot have been asked to do this movement before the hindquarters are strong enough. Rather than stepping the hind legs under his body the horse will step to the side to avoid taking sufficient weight on the hindquarters and to avoid bending the joints of the hind legs. Once established this can be a very difficult habit to break.

Go back to getting correct lengthening, and then medium, trot, gradually strengthening the hindquarters before attempting extension again.

## Wrong Lead

*In canter*
The rider must learn to 'feel' whether the horse is on the correct lead, not look down for it.

Clear and concise aids need to be given for the strike-off so that there can be no confusion on the part of the horse. Having bent the horse to the direction towards which you wish to strike off, place the outside leg just behind the girth and the inside leg on the girth. If the strike-off is wrong, the horse must be brought straight back to walk or trot and the exercise repeated. If a horse has difficulty on one lead, it may be necessary for a short while to take a 'wrong flexion' to block the outside shoulder and free the inside one. Once the horse has accepted the correct lead, the bend towards the leading leg should be regained.

# CHAPTER 5

# School Movements

It is important that riders learn to execute the school figures correctly and accurately. Circles must be of the exact size required, starting and finishing precisely where the test demands. Turning and tracking to left and right must be shown with correct bend, balance and impulsion. Transitions must be ridden accurately to the markers. Many marks are lost in competition through sloppy riding of the figures.

Having stressed the importance of accuracy, I must say that the first consideration of the rider must be the preserving of the correct gaits of the horse and the acceptance of the aids. As the horse progresses with his training the rider's ability to ride an accurate test should improve. It is important that the rider 'uses' the school movements to increase the engagement, impulsion and suppleness of the horse, and does not just 'perform' them as tricks.

## Circles

The circle is probably the most useful and most used of all the school movements. The most usual sizes ridden are 20, 15 and 10 metres. Circles of between 6 and 10 metres are described as Voltes, and these can be properly performed only by a horse that is in an advanced stage of training. In walk and trot the horse should be bent to

the direction of the circle, in canter to the direction of the leading leg.

Circles are often ridden badly, to an odd shape or the wrong size. It is important to visualize the shape, and then look ahead to see exactly where to go next.

*Rider looking well ahead to gauge the circle.*

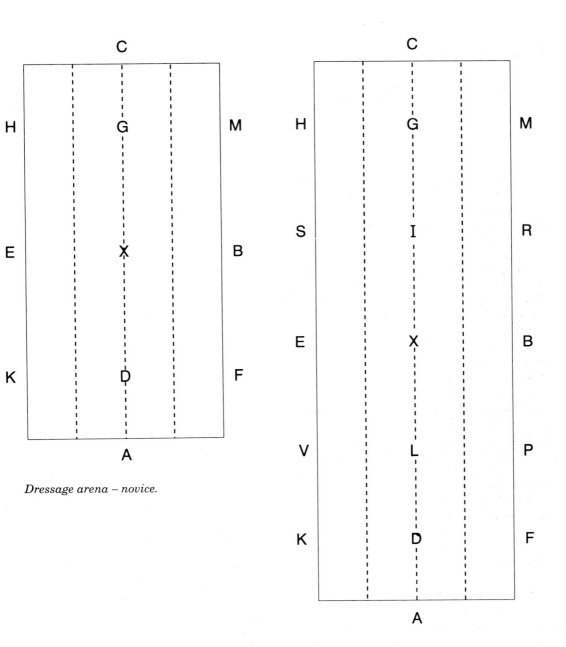

*Dressage arena – novice.*

*Dressage arena – advanced.*

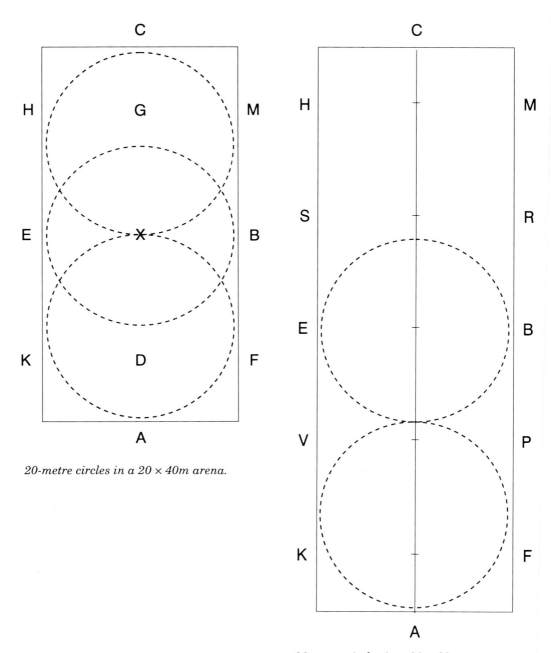

*20-metre circles in a 20 × 40m arena.*

*20-metre circles in a 20 × 60m arena.*

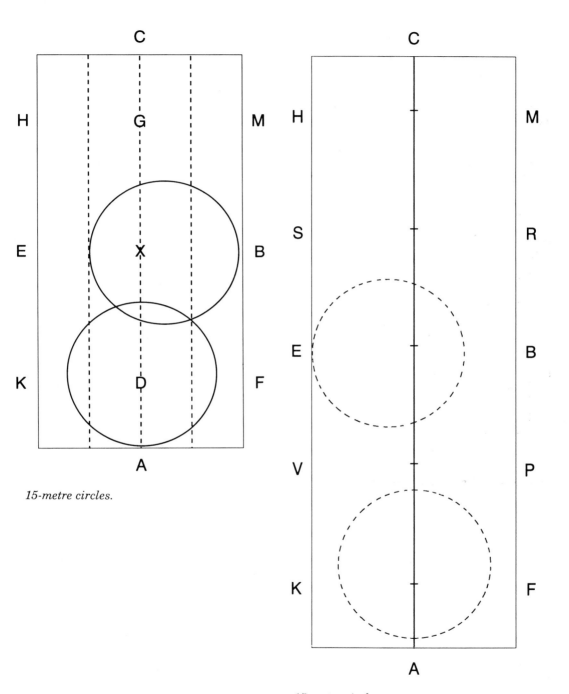

*15-metre circles.*

*15-metre circles.*

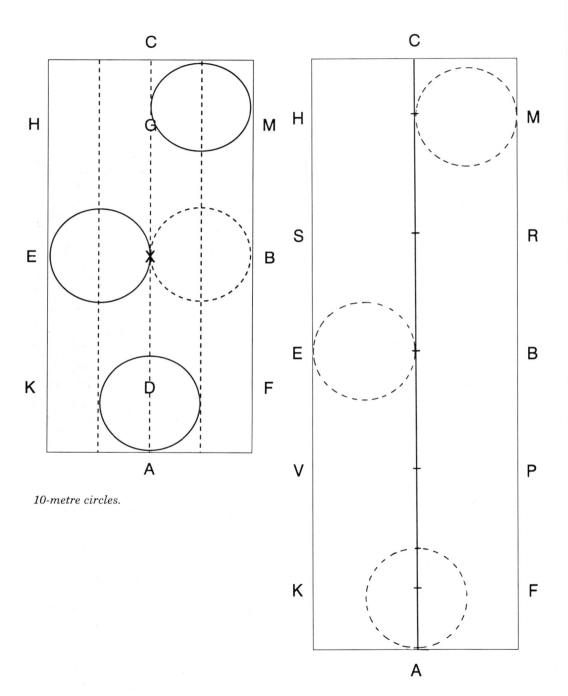

*10-metre circles.*

*10-metre circles.*

## Faults

### *Falling onto Inside Shoulder*

If the horse is falling onto the inside shoulder on a circle, it will be because the rider has taken insufficient inside bend and is not using the inside leg to good enough effect.

### *Falling onto Outside Shoulder*

If a horse falls onto the outside shoulder on a circle, it indicates that the rider has failed to exert sufficient control with his

*Horse and rider unbalanced.*

*Falling in on a circle.*

outside rein. The horse will feel unbalanced and will find it difficult to get round the circle. The shape of the circle will not be round. The horse may look as if more weight is being taken by the legs on the outside of the circle and he will almost certainly be too bent to the inside.

This problem is usually associated with the horse's having too much bend to the inside. With the outside rein against the horse's neck, you should endeavour to keep him straighter, sometimes even bent a little to the outside until control over the shoulder has been regained. Once this has

*Good bend on a circle.*

*Flexion in preparation for a turn.*

*Tilting head to evade the true bend.*

been achieved the true flexion may once again be taken.

## Head Unsteadiness

An unsteady head may be caused either by the rider's hands being unsteady or by the horse not truly accepting the bit. If the problem is the rider's he must work hard to keep the hands still but at the same time making sure that they are not set.

Unsteady hands are often the result of a weak seat. This is best strengthened through riding without reins and stirrups on the lunge. The horse that is not truly accepting the bit must be taught to do so: you must 'feel and give', on the hard side of the horse's mouth and keep an even contact on the other side until the horse gives to the hand; at the same time the seat and legs must be used to keep the horse going forwards.

## Hollow Back

A horse that hollows his back on a circle is

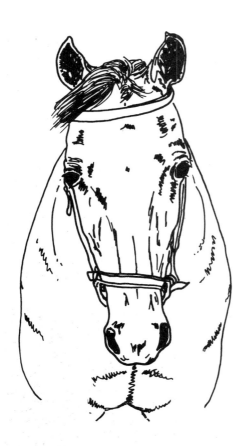

*Head tilting.*

horse is hollow through all his work, and not just on circles, it may be of help to work him with his head and neck very low for a while to strengthen him over his topline, but when doing this be careful not to put him on the forehand.

## *Lacking Bend*

The horse should be bent uniformly to the line of the circle. If the horse lacks bend it is usually the fault of the rider's inside leg.

usually trying to avoid the rider's contact with the mouth and also avoid stepping under enough with his inside hind leg.

When a horse hollows, he has the appearance of being dish-shaped, which the rider should be able to feel from the fact that the head is up and the muscles of the horse's back are held stiffly.

Work initially on 20-metre circles and concentrate on gaining acceptance of the aids and better engagement of the hindquarters. (Young horses should not be asked to work on smaller circles until their hindquarters are strong enough.) If the

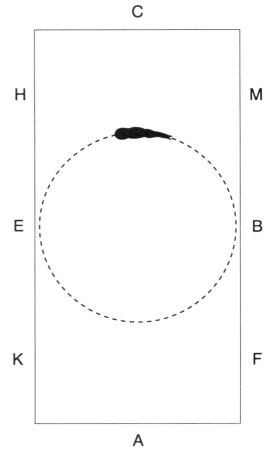

*Horse uniformly bent.*

To remedy the problem, consider whether your aids are clear. Direct the horse on to the line of the circle with the inside rein just away from the horse's neck; the outside rein should be against the horse's neck to control the amount of bend, the outside shoulder and the impulsion. The inside leg, on the girth, creates and maintains the impulsion and is the 'pillar' for the horse to bend around. Your outside leg, just behind the girth, assists with the bend and controls the hindquarters.

## Overbent

A horse that is overbent has stopped going forwards from the rider's leg aids and has dropped the contact with the rider's hands. His nose is behind the vertical.

If this is happening only on circles it is probably because the rider is being too strong with the inside rein, and it can therefore be quite easily corrected by using more inside leg and less inside rein. If the problem is occurring throughout the work it will be a lot harder to correct. When the horse drops the contact, you should take up the slack in the rein and drive the horse forwards with strong seat and leg aids. Once the horse has accepted the contact, you can then lighten it, but you should not give it away. Many riders make the mistake of dropping the contact

*Horse overbent, caused by the tension of the curb rein.*

*Rider looking down and collapsing the back, causing the horse to overbend and go on the forehand.*

in the hope that the horse will take his nose forwards, but this is a grave mistake because the dropping of the contact is precisely what the horse is seeking by going overbent. The horse must learn to accept the contact of the rider through the reins and respond to the leg to go forwards.

## Poor-Shaped Circles

It is the rider's responsibility to make the figures a good shape whether at home or in competition. At all times the rider must get into the habit of riding the movements correctly and accurately.

## Quarters In

On a circle the horse's hind feet must

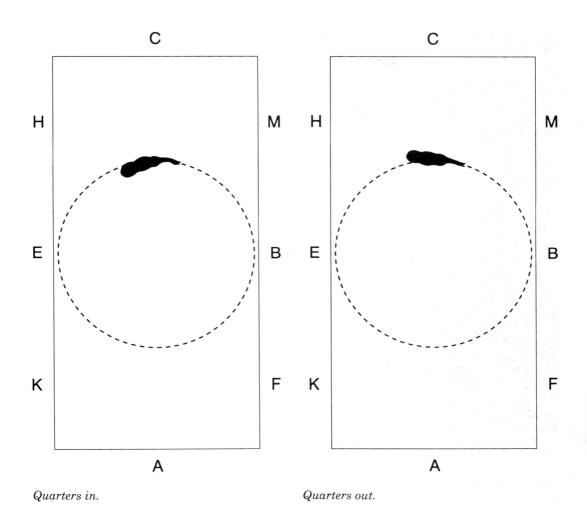

Quarters in.

Quarters out.

follow the tracks of the forefeet; any deviation from this will be a fault and must be corrected before it becomes an established habit.

Do not attempt to put the quarters out, but rather ride the horse more strongly forwards into the outside rein. Do make sure that your outside leg is not too far back or too strong, thus causing the problem. It is also a good idea to take a slight shoulder-fore position, which will ensure that the forehand is under control, which will encourage the hindquarters to follow it.

## Quarters Out

On a circle the horse's hind feet must follow the tracks of his forefeet. The hindquarters of the horse should be controlled by the rider's outside leg placed just behind the girth.

*The neck is bent too much to the leading leg.*

Quite often this fault occurs because the rider has asked for too much bend in the neck. Make sure that the 'outside aids' are correctly in place, and if so use the schooling whip to back up the outside leg.

## Stiffness

If the horse shows stiffness on the circle, while having no physical reason to do so , he will need to be made more supple and responsive to the rider's aids.

In the younger horse that is not ready for collection the leg-yielding exercises should help, and in the more trained horse leg-yielding and shoulder-in exercises should both be used. You must aim to make the horse equally supple to both sides.

## Too Big

Care must be taken to ride circles the correct size in the arena, and to do this the rider will need to become more accurate in everyday riding.

Many riders try for accuracy only on the day of the show and are not particular enough at home. You must ensure that the horse is advanced enough in his training to perform the size of circle that you are asking for. Young horses should not be asked to perform very small circles until their hindquarters are strong enough.

## Too Small

The rider must be careful to ride the circles accurately. Sometimes the horse makes the circle too small by falling in against the rider's inside leg. If this is the case, you must use a more effective aid and back it up with the schooling whip if necessary. As with any circle, you must know clearly what you are aiming for and concentrate on getting the right shape.

## Wrong Bend

If the horse is bent the wrong way on a circle he is not adhering to the basic principles of dressage. The only time it is acceptable for the horse to be bent away from the direction of the circle is in counter-canter, when he should be bent towards the leading leg.

Both the rider's hands and legs are needed to teach the horse to bend

*Horse bent to the right before a circle. The rider's right leg is too far back.*

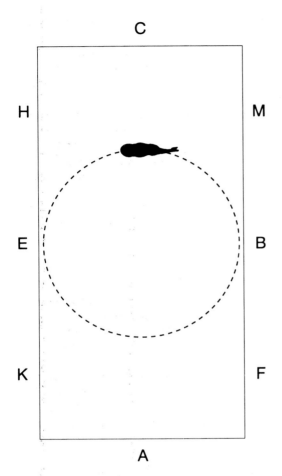

*Wrong bend an circle.*

horses are one-sided, that is to say they find it easier to bend one way than the other. Do not work only on the difficult side but work to straighten the horse on the hollow side and to gain more bend on the stiff side. In this way you will learn to have the aids correctly placed on the horse.

## Loops

Loops can be ridden in walk, trot and canter on the long side of the arena or from the centre line. In walk and trot, the bend must be changed with each change of direction, but in canter the bend must be maintained to the leading leg. Loops may be ridden at varying degrees of difficulty: just a metre or two in from the track to start with, increasing the depth of the loop as the horse's training progresses. Riding a loop is one of the best ways to introduce the young horse to counter-canter.

## Faults

### *Loops Too Shallow*

A loop that is too shallow is really the result of rider error. Care must be taken to ride the figures as laid down on the test sheet. Most loops will be required to be 3 or 5 metres in from B or E, and you must learn to judge these distances accurately.

### *Loss of Bend in Counter-Canter*

If the loop is to be ridden in canter the bend must be maintained to the leading leg throughout the movement, unlike in walk or trot where the bend is changed

correctly. Your inside hand should be used, just away from the horse's neck, to give the direction of the circle and to ask for the flexion to the inside. The outside hand, against the horse's neck, will control the amount of bend, the impulsion and the horse's outside shoulder. Your inside leg, placed on the girth, will create impulsion and bend; the outside leg, placed just behind the girth, will help to bend the horse and control the hindquarters. Most

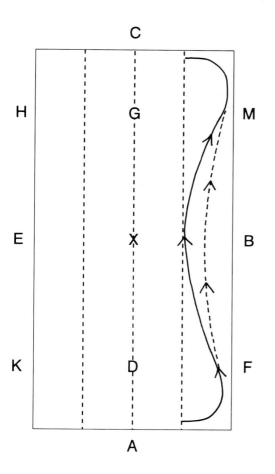

*Loops.*

counter-canter on the return to the track is minimal.

The rhythm and tempo of the canter must stay the same throughout. You must keep the aids in place so that the horse realizes that he must stay on the same lead and keep the weight a little over the inside leg. As the horse gets stronger and is able to maintain his balance, the loops may be made deeper to increase the difficulty of the counter-canter. Although the horse must remain bent in the counter-canter he must stay on one track and not be pushed sideways onto two tracks on the return to the track.

## On Two Tracks

In the return to the track, especially in canter where this fault often occurs, the rider must be careful not to allow the horse to swing his quarters and return on two tracks.

Make sure that the canter aids are kept in place throughout the movement. Taking a shoulder-fore position will give better control and help to prevent the hindquarters from falling in.

## Resistance to Change of Bend

Resistance to the change of bend usually occurs as a result of lack of preparation by the rider before the change of direction.

For a 5-metre loop ridden on the long side of the arena from H to K, and after leaving the corner by H with correct bend, you should for a moment straighten the horse then take a flexion to the new direction before commencing the turn. Once you are heading back towards H, the horse should again be straightened before the new flexion is taken to make the turn on

with each change of direction. The amount of bend required in the counter-canter is the same as that required for the true canter, so no difference is shown in the amount of bend throughout the movement. The loop, ridden on the long side of the arena, is an ideal place to teach the young horse counter-canter in the early stages of training. At first the rider can ask the horse to come just a metre or two in from B or E so that the amount of to the track. No sudden changes of bend should be made and a turn should not be commenced before the horse has bent to the new direction.

## Serpentines

The serpentine consists of half-circles connected by a straight line (*see* the diagram). The size of the half-circles determines the length of the straight connection . A serpentine may be ridden in walk, trot or canter. In walk and trot the bend must be shown to the direction of the half-circle; in canter the bend is maintained to the leading leg. The serpentine is a useful exercise to assess the horse's suppleness, acceptance of the aids, and ability to stay in balance during the changes of direction. As the horse becomes more collected as his training progresses, more half-circles may be fitted into the arena.

## Faults

### *Badly Placed Simple Changes*

Some dressage tests require the rider to perform a serpentine in canter with simple changes on the centre line. A simple change is canter–walk–canter. At the lower levels, the downward transition to walk may be progressive: canter–trot, walk–canter. Medium level and above demands that both transitions are direct. In a simple change, three or four clear walk strides should be shown (not jogging steps), and the movement looks so much better if these steps are placed in a balanced way over the centre line. This is

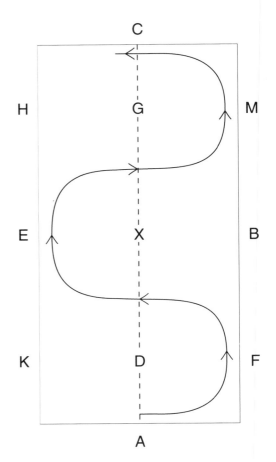

*Serpentines.*

something that takes a lot of practice and riders must ensure that the quality of the canter is not compromised for the sake of the accuracy. Only regular practice at home will remedy badly placed changes.

### *Changes not on Centre Line*

More advanced tests require serpentines to be shown at the canter with flying changes on the centre line. It can take a lot of practice to achieve this without spoiling the canter or restricting the flying changes. The quality of the collection and the expression of the changes must take precedence over the accuracy but, having said that, practice will enable you to achieve both.

## Loops Uneven

Each loop or half-circle of the serpentine must be of the same size, and it is up to the rider to learn to ride these correctly.

It is always a good plan when you have a test to ride that includes a serpentine to draw it out on paper first and work out the points at which you must touch the track and cross the centre line.

## Poor Preparation

To make the changes of direction smoothly and correctly the rider needs to prepare the horse before each turn commences. Approaching the centre line the horse should be straightened for a moment and the new flexion taken just after passing over the line and before the next turn.

A good exercise to prepare for this is to trot on a straight line and practise flexing the horse one way for a few strides and then to the other direction without deviating from the straight line.

## Quarters Swinging

The hind feet of the horse should follow the tracks of the forefeet throughout the serpentine.

In an effort to 'show the bend' on the half-circles riders often take too much with the inside rein and lose control over the outside of the horse. The rider's outside leg must control the hindquarters of the horse, and the outside rein the amount of bend, the shoulder and the impulsion.

*In Counter-Canter*

Some serpentines demand that a loop of the serpentine shall be ridden in counter-canter.

Often the horse's quarters swing because the rider, in an attempt to prevent the horse from changing leg, overuses the outside leg, which pushes the horse's hindquarters to the inside. As a result, the hind feet do not follow the path of the forefeet. To correct this problem, it is important to practise maintaining counter-canter without overusing the outside leg.

## Rhythm Varied

Throughout the serpentine the horse should maintain the same rhythm and impulsion.

Varied rhythm often results from the rider's effort to show a clear change of bend when crossing the centre line, and in so doing restricting the horse's forward movement and momentarily changing the rhythm of the steps. More novice riders might find it a help to count the 'one–two' rhythm of the trot to themselves whilst riding the movement to make sure that the rhythm does not alter.

## Half-Circles

Half-circles are ridden from various positions in the arena and follow the same criteria as circles. The horse must stay in balance and in rhythm. In walk and trot the horse is bent to the direction in which

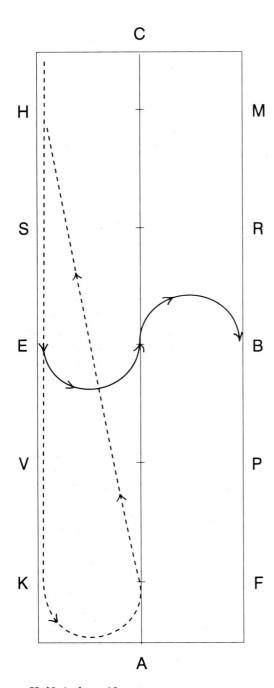

*Half-circles – 10 metres.*

he is travelling, and in canter he is bent towards the leading leg.

## Faults

### *Flat Half-Circle*

It is a good idea for the more novice rider to draw on a piece of paper all the movements of the test that is to be ridden. This will give the rider a clear picture of what is required. If a 10-metre half-circle is to be ridden from E to X, the rider must touch a point 5 metres from the diameter line (*see* diagram).

Sometimes the half-circles are flat because the horse has not remained correctly bent round the rider's inside leg and has fallen into the half-circle. A more effective inside leg will need to be used in this case.

### *Loss of Impulsion*

In all the school figures – circles, serpentines or half-circles – the horse must maintain the same amount of impulsion and engagement.

Most often the impulsion is lost because the rider is too concerned about the accuracy of the movement and not enough about the horse's way of going. Only practice will enable the rider to ride correct figures and at the same time keep the horse moving forwards properly.

### *Loss of Rhythm*

As with the loss of impulsion, loss of rhythm can occur because the rider's concentrating too much on the accuracy of the movement disturbs the horse's rhythm. Daily practice of correct figure riding will make the rider more confident to think more of how the horse is performing and less about the movement itself.

## Overshot Centre Line

Half-circles ridden from the side of the arena to the centre line are very obvious to the judge if they are either too small or too large.

As in all circle or half-circle riding, you must look ahead to the point at which you want to touch the centre line or the side of the arena. You must also check that you are not taking too much bend to the inside and consequently losing control over the horse's outside shoulder and hindquarters.

## Changes of Rein

Changes of rein (changes of direction) may be ridden on the diagonal, on the centre line, across the arena (E–B), by a half-circle or within a circle. In walk and trot the horse should change the bend when changing direction; in canter he should remain bent towards the leading leg. The rider should take care to 'prepare' for the change of direction, keep the same impulsion and rhythm, and control the horse's shoulders and hindquarters.

## Faults

### Loss of Bend

At walk or trot on the diagonal line the horse should be straight, but in canter the horse should remain bent to the leading leg until a simple change, flying change or transition to walk or trot is asked for. If the canter is required to be held for the duration of the diagonal line the bend must not fail as the horse approaches the end of the line.

Many horses anticipating the new direction will try to straighten themselves, so you must keep the aids in place and concentrate on controlling the bend.

## Lost Outside Shoulder

The losing of the outside shoulder occurs mainly in the turn on to the diagonal line, when the rider uses too much inside rein to make the turn and not enough outside rein and leg, allowing the horse to 'drift' on up the track.

If this has become an established habit you may, for a short while, need to practise turning on to the diagonal line with a 'wrong' bend in order to control the outside shoulder. Once control has been gained the exercise can once more be ridden with correct bend.

## Not Straight

Once the horse has completed the turn on to the diagonal line he should be straight until bend is needed for the turn at the other end.

Many riders omit to straighten the horse after the turn on to the diagonal and instead keep the bend all the way across. This is not only incorrect but may cause irregular steps if the horse is in medium or extended trot. If the diagonal is being ridden in canter, a flexion to the leading leg will be maintained but the horse must still be straight: the hind feet must follow in the tracks of the forefeet.

## *Wandering*

This is a term that would most often apply in walk although it can be seen in trot and canter.

Having completed the turn on to the diagonal line you must set your eye on the marker that you are riding towards and ride to it in a purposeful manner. Many horses and riders take the walking part of the test as a rest period, but this is a mistake: many marks are lost as a result.

## Straight Lines

The ability to ride the horse in a straight line at walk, trot and canter is of the utmost importance and can be achieved only if the horse is equally supple to both sides. At canter the horse will be required to have a slight flexion to the leading leg but he must still remain on one track, the hind feet following in the tracks of the forefeet.

Many riders do not seem to be able to tell if the horse is straight. A good start is to give concentration to the whole of the horse's forehand making sure that the shoulders, neck and head are aligned. If this is achieved, the hindquarters will follow.

*Very straight but overbent.*

## Faults

### *Head Weaving*

In an attempt to keep the horse's head 'down', many riders cause the head to 'weave' from side to side. This is most obvious to the judge on the centre line but it is incorrect at all times.

You must concentrate on using the hands in the correct manner. If this becomes an established habit the horse will continue to do it even when the rider keeps the hands still, so it is important that you concentrate on using your hands in the correct manner.

## *Off Centre*

Riders sometimes make the turn on to the centre line without looking far enough ahead.

When riding towards the corner by F or K for a turn on to the centre line, look towards D to make a correct turn, not towards A. As soon as the turn on to the line begins, look towards C. In this way you will arrive on the line and be able to stay on it.

## Quarters to Left or Right

At all times on a straight line the horse's hind feet should follow in the tracks of the forefeet. At canter a slight flexion will be asked for towards the leading leg but the horse will still be on one track. A horse is able to travel straight only if he is equally supple to both sides. When a horse has his quarters to one side on a straight line he is usually bent that way in his neck also.

Do not try just to push the hindquarters back to the line, instead straighten the horse's neck with the rein and, with the legs, ride more strongly forwards. Your outside leg should be behind the girth to control the hindquarters but should not need to be used with much pressure to keep the horse straight.

## Wandering

If a horse is wandering off the straight line it usually indicates that he is lacking sufficient forward impulsion and activity.

Keep your eye on the marker towards which you are heading and ride in a more purposeful way towards it, keeping the hand and leg aids firmly in place.

## Simple Changes

Simple changes are always ridden through walk. If walk steps are not required the movement is described as a

*Hindquarters to left on a straight line.*

change of leg through trot. Up to and including elementary standard, the downward transition may be progressive (canter–trot–walk), but the upward transition must be direct (walk–canter). At medium standard and above, both the upward and downward transitions must be direct: canter–walk–canter. The rider must be sure to show three or four clear walk steps and not just 'jogging' steps.

## Faults

### *No Clear Walk Shown*

Several steps of walk should be shown between the two canters during a simple change of leg, and they must be clear, straight and without tension. Jogging steps will not be counted as walk.

### *Not Direct*

In tests of medium standard and above, both transitions must be direct and not show any trot strides. In lower standard tests the downward transition may be shown through trot.

To be able to walk from canter the horse must be well engaged from behind and in good balance. As with nearly all transitions that go wrong it is not the transition that needs working on but the gait before it. To produce a good transition from canter to walk the horse must be in good balance, with the hocks well engaged, and he must be accepting the rider's aids. To be able to canter from walk, the walk must be active and forwards and the horse attentive to the rider's aids. You must practise these transitions until they are smooth. If you continue to experience difficulty, consider whether your aids are as clear as they should be.

### *Not Straight*

Throughout the simple change the horse should remain on a straight line, the hind feet following in the tracks of the forefeet. In canter the horse will have a slight flexion to the leading leg; as he comes to walk the rider will straighten him out and then take a slight flexion in preparation for the strike-off but at no time should he deviate from the straight line.

### *Resistance*

All transitions should be shown straight, in balance, and free from resistance.

The cause of resistance in a transition is usually lack of preparation on the part of the rider. Prior to the simple change, you must ensure that the horse is collected and in good balance. If the horse is on the forehand or lacking balance in any way he will not be able to make a correct transition to walk; the same applies for the transition to canter. The horse must be forward and active and responsive to the aids.

## Giving and Retaking the Reins

This movement requires the rider to push both hands forwards to release the contact with the horse's mouth and then to retake it. This should be one continuous movement. This is one of the most useful training exercises for indicating to the rider or judge whether the horse is able to stay in balance, without the support of the rider's hands. It also clearly shows the horse's acceptance of the bit as the rein is retaken. It is important that the giving and retaking of the rein is a continuous movement, the contact not being given away for too many strides. Throughout the movement the horse must remain straight, in balance, and show no resistance to the retaking of the rein.

# Faults

## Contact Not Released

This movement clearly requires that the rider must release the contact and failure to do so will result in the loss of many marks. It is necessary to show that the horse is able to remain in balance, be straight, and not increase speed when the rein is given and that he will accept the retaking of the rein without resistance.

## Head High

As the rider releases the contact the horse should remain in a round outline; if he lifts his head he will also hollow his back. This movement is designed to show that the horse's head is not held in place by the rider's hands. If the position of the head changes at all it should be down and forwards to seek the hand, never upward. Because the movement is continuous the horse's head should basically stay where it was.

Make sure that the horse is on the bit and alert to the aids before attempting the movement. To begin with, the give and retake can be practised on a circle where it is easier to remain in control, but once the horse is working correctly you should be able to perform the movement anywhere in the arena at walk, trot or canter. When teaching the horse to accept this exercise it may be helpful to practise giving only on the inside rein until he is confident that nothing untoward will happen.

## Loss of Balance

During the whole movement, and in fact through all his work, the horse should be able to remain in balance without the support of the rider's hands. The giving and retaking of the reins is a good test to see whether this is possible. When the reins are given the horse should not increase speed, drop on to the forehand, deviate from the straight line or show any loss of balance. If a loss of balance occurs the rider must be aware that he is allowing the horse to balance on his hands.

Use half-halts to engage the horse more from behind so that he is able to carry himself without support from the hands. It is important that the giving and retaking is ridden as a continuous movement: if the contact is given away for too long the horse will have to lower his head and neck to seek the reins, and this is not required in this movement.

## Not Straight

The horse should not deviate from the straight line during the giving and retaking of the reins. He should be sufficiently balanced and controlled by the rider's seat and leg aids to remain straight.

If this fault is apparent when performing this movement, it must be assumed that the horse is being kept straight by the reins alone, in which case you need to rethink your horse's general schooling.

## Reins Given for Too Long

This movement demands that the giving and retaking of the reins is a continuous

*Rider pulling on the reins and shortening the horse's neck.*

movement, so the rider's hands should not stay forwards for too long. If the contact is released for too long we would expect the horse to lower his head and neck to seek the hand. This is not required in this movement. If, when the reins are given for too long, the horse remains in the same outline it is apparent that the horse is then effectively behind the bit.

## Resistance

Resistance is often shown in the retaking of the rein.

Take care not to snatch at the rein but to retake the contact gently but firmly, keeping both legs in place to keep him forwards. Repeat the exercise until the horse accepts the contact being taken back.

## Rushing

The rhythm, tempo and speed of the gait should remain the same throughout the giving and retaking of the reins. If the horse rushes as the reins are given it shows that he was not correctly between the rider's hands and legs before the movement.

Use half-halts to improve the horse's balance and practise the exercise on a circle until control can be maintained.

---

**Rules for Riding School Movements**

- Be clear in your own mind as to what the movement should look like. If unsure, draw it on a piece of paper before riding it.
- Ride with accuracy daily, not just when competing.
- Always put the purity of the horse's gaits over the accuracy of the movement.
- Use the movements to improve the horse's way of going, not just to be performed as tricks.

# CHAPTER 6

# Halts

## The Correct Halt

At the halt, the horse should stand attentive, motionless and straight, with the weight evenly distributed over all four legs, which should be quite square. The neck should be raised, the poll high, and the nose slightly in front of the vertical. While remaining on the bit, and maintaining a light and soft contact with the rider's hand, the horse should be ready to move off at the slightest indication of the rider.

The rider should sit up and sit still, keep his legs close to the horse's sides, and keep the rein contact even.

## Faults

### Anticipation

The transition to or from the halt must not be anticipated by the horse. If the horse anticipates the halt from walk, trot or canter he should be ridden briskly forwards. If he anticipates moving forwards from the halt before the rider has applied the aids to do so, the halt must be re-established and the horse made to wait for the command to go forwards.

If the horse habitually anticipates, vary the duration of the halt, or the point at which you ask for halt, during practice sessions; so this will prevent his being able to predict the precise movement of halt or moving forward from halt.

### Falling onto Left/Right Shoulder

The horse must come to, and leave, the halt straight and without any deviation from the straight line. Neither the shoulders nor hindquarters of the horse should move to left or right. The rider must ensure that the horse is straight and between the hand and leg before the halt. A half-halt may be applied just before the halt to test this.

Crooked halts frequently occur because the horse was not straight or on the bit enough just prior to the halt. If the rider is not sitting squarely in the saddle, the extra weight on one side will encourage the horse to step in that direction.

### Inattention

The horse should remain on the bit at the halt and attentive to the rider's aids, ready to move forwards or backwards from the lightest of aids from the rider. Although halts should never be rushed, the young horse should not be required to halt for too long as he will lose concentration.

*A good halt.*

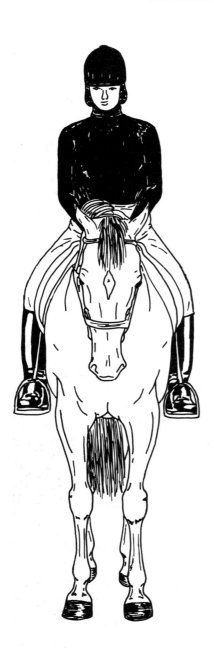

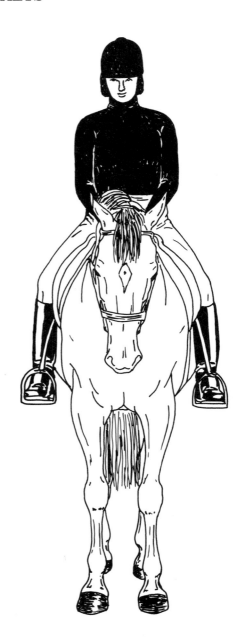

*Rider at halt legs on.*

*Rider at halt legs off.*

## Moving at Halt

The horse must remain stationary at the halt, until the rider gives the aids to move forwards or back.

Quite often, a horse will move at the halt because the rider has not made sure that the halt was balanced and square in the first place. Once the halt is established the rider must sit square and still in the saddle so that the horse's balance is not disturbed. Make sure that you are not inadvertently giving your horse an instruction to move. Ensure that the aids for halt are clear.

## No Immobility

When the horse is at the halt he should show complete immobility. Many horses fidget, moving forwards or back with one or more legs.

Do not be tempted to take the aids off to cure this problem as you will then lose even more control over the horse. The horse must learn to stand still at the halt with the rider's aids in place. If the horse is young or nervous, talking to him at the halt will help him to relax and stand still. However, the voice must not be used during a competition.

## Not Square

The horse should halt with his weight evenly distributed over all four legs. If the horse is not standing square he will not be able to do this.

*The halt is not square, and the rider is tipping forwards.*

*In this picture the rider has contact with her horse's mouth but her legs are not in contact with his sides.*

*This picture illustrates a hollow outline and the horse is above the bit. In dressage tests, martingales are not allowed.*

Most halts that are not square come about because the rider has made the transition to the halt too abruptly. You must learn to feel all four feet of the horse as they come into place, not just stop the horse mid-stride. If the horse continually leaves one leg behind (usually a hind leg), you may need to use the schooling whip gently on that side to make the horse bring the leg forward. The horse should always make a square halt by stepping each leg forwards, never back.

## Not Straight

To be able to make a straight halt the horse must be in balance in his gait before the transition. The horse must be between the rider's hands and legs, attentive to the aids.

If the horse comes to the halt not straight, he should be made to take a step forwards to straighten himself, never pushed to the side or taken backwards. Make sure that you have an even contact on both sides of the horse's mouth and that both legs are on with equal pressure.

## Reluctant Move-Off

The horse should move forwards from the halt at the lightest of signals from the rider.

*The horse is off the bit through lack of contact. The martingale would not be allowed in a test.*

*Too much rein tension, causing the horse to put his head up and hollow.*

If the horse is slow to move off, back up the leg aids with the schooling whip. A young horse should not be expected to halt for long periods of time as he will lose concentration. If the horse has halted correctly and remained on the aids the move off should not create a problem.

## Resistance

At the halt the rider must keep the horse on the bit and between hand and leg, ready to move forwards or backwards at the lightest signal.

Do not allow resistance from the horse to blackmail you into slackening off the contact with the mouth or the legs. If the horse shows resistance to the hand or leg aids, increase the pressure; do not decrease it.

## Resting Hind Leg

At the halt, the horse must have his weight evenly distributed over all four legs. This is not possible if the horse is resting a hind leg.

As soon as you feel the horse taking the weight off one leg, push him forwards and then re-establish the halt.

## Stepping Back

A square halt must always be achieved by

the horse stepping forwards, never back. The horse must remain collected at the halt and if he puts a hind leg back this collection will be lost as will the ability to move forwards correctly.

The moment you feel the horse step back, send him forwards and then re-establish the halt. Although you must keep a light contact with the horse's mouth during the halt, do make sure that it is not an over-strong contact that is causing the horse to step back.

### Rules for a Good Halt

- A good halt can only come about from a balanced gait.
- The aids must be kept in 'place' during the halt.
- A good contact can only be achieved with an 'elastic' arm.
- Halts should be made square by stepping forward, never back.
- Do not continually practise halts at 'X' or the horse will anticipate them.
- Make sure that your weight is central in the saddle with equal weight on both stirrups.

# CHAPTER 7

# Lateral Work

In all the lateral movements, the horse is slightly bent and moves with the forehand and the hindquarters on two different tracks. Bending or flexion at the poll and neck has repercussions on the whole spine, so the bend or flexion should never be exaggerated so that it impairs the balance and fluency of the movement concerned: this applies especially to the half-pass, where the bend should be less evident than in the shoulder-in, travers and renvers.

During all the lateral movements the gait should remain free and regular; it must be maintained by constant impulsion but it must be supple, cadenced and balanced. At all the lateral movements the side to which the horse should be bent is the inside. The opposite side is the outside.

## Leg-Yield

During the leg-yield the horse is straight, except for a slight bend at the poll, so that the rider is just able to see the horse's eyebrow and nostril on the inside. The horse's inside legs pass and cross in front of the outside legs: the horse is looking away from the direction in which he is moving. The leg-yield is the most basic of all the lateral movements and should actually be included in the training of the horse before he is ready for collected work.

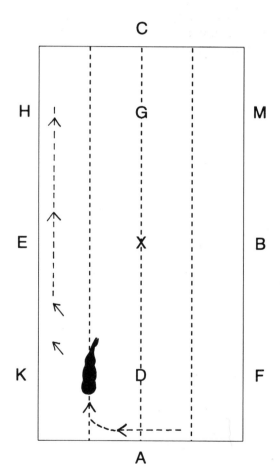

*Leg yielding.*

*A fair leg-yield. However, the rider's left leg should be further back to control the hindquarters.*

*The leg-yield with the rider's legs better positioned.*

The leg-yielding can be performed on the diagonal line, in which case the horse should be as near possible parallel to the long sides of the arena. It can also be performed along the wall, in which case the horse should be at an angle of about 35 degrees to the direction in which he is moving.

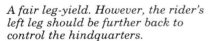

*Rules for Good Leg-Yielding*

- The purity of the trot must be maintained throughout the movement.
- The movement should be ridden to gain more collection, engagement and suppleness, not as a 'trick'.
- The horse should have a slight

flexion at the poll, not a uniform bend as in the other lateral movements.
- Any loss of impulsion during the leg-yielding exercise should be countered by sending the horse forwards and, only once the impul-

**Faults Commonly Occurring in Leg-Yield**

- Falling onto Outside Shoulder
- Loss of Impulsion
- Quarters Leading
- Quarters Trailing
- Too Much Bend

sion has been regained, the exercise restarted.

- The horse's forehand should at all times during the exercise be slightly in advance of the hindquarters.
- Leg-yielding should be practised equally on both reins.

# Shoulder-In

At the shoulder-in, the horse should be slightly bent round the inside leg of the rider. The horse's inside foreleg passes and crosses in front of the outside leg: the horse should look away from the direction in which he is moving. The shoulder-in is a suppling and collecting movement. Shoulder-in is performed along the wall, at an angle of about 30 degrees to the direction in which the horse is moving. To ask for the shoulder-in, the rider places the inside leg on the girth to ask for the bend and maintain the impulsion, while the outside leg, just behind the girth, controls the hindquarters. A slightly open inside rein leads the forehand in from the track, and the outside rein against the horse's neck controls the amount of bend, the impulsion and the outside shoulder.

This exercise is invaluable for gaining control over the horse's forehand. Also to a minor degree, the shoulder-in position or shoulder-fore is constantly used to aid straightening in all gaits. Even if the rider merely 'thinks' shoulder-in, the aids used will provide him with better control.

*Rules for Good Shoulder-In*

- The shoulder-in exercise should be used to supple, collect and engage the hindquarters.

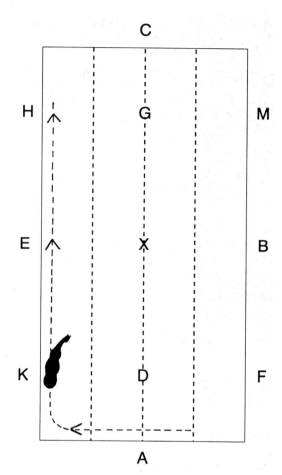

*Shoulder-in.*

- Shoulder-in must be started by bringing the horse's shoulders in, not pushing the hindquarters out.
- The trot should be enhanced by the riding of shoulder-in, not marred.
- There is no value in riding the shoulder-in on more than three tracks.
- Shoulder-in should be pratised equally on both reins.

*Shoulder-in on four, rather than three, tracks.*

- If the shoulder-in begins to fail, the rider is best advised to circle away, regain the lost bend or impulsion, and then begin the exercise again.

| **Faults Commonly Occurring in Shoulder-In** |
| --- |
| • Angle Varied<br>• Loss of Angle<br>• Loss of Bend<br>• Loss of Impulsion<br>• Quarters Out<br>• Too Little Angle<br>• Too Much Angle<br>• Too Much Neck Bend |

## Half-Pass

Half-pass is a variation of travers, executed on the diagonal instead of along the wall. The horse, slightly bent round the rider's inside leg, should be as parallel as possible to the long sides of the arena, although the forehand should be slightly in advance of the quarters. The horse's outside legs pass and cross in front of the inside legs. The horse is looking in the direction in which he is moving. He should

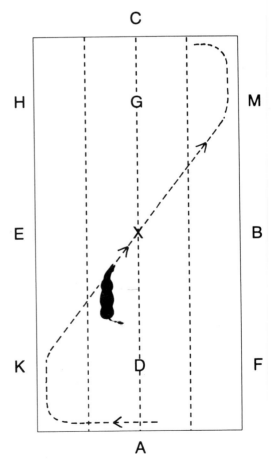

*Half-pass.*

*Open inside rein.*

*Inside rein into neck.*

maintain the same cadence and balance throughout the whole movement. The half-pass may be performed in walk, trot, canter or *passage*. The rider bends the horse to the marker towards which he is travelling with his inside leg on the girth to create and maintain the bend and impulsion. The outside rein controls the amount of bend, the outside shoulder and the impulsion. The rider's outside leg, behind the girth, asks the quarters to move over.

### Rules for Riding Good Half-Pass

- The half-pass should be practised equally on both reins.

- The forehand should always be slightly in advance of the hindquarters.
- The purity of the gaits should be enhanced by the half-passes, not diminished.
- The amount of bend in the half-pass should be governed by the steepness of the movement. The horse should look towards the marker towards which he is travelling, so more bend will be required in a steep half-pass than in a longer one.
- The rider should have his weight slightly in the direction of the half-pass not away from it.

*A fair half-pass to the left, but the rider is leaning away from the movement.*

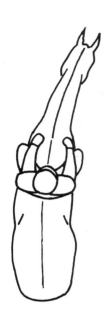

*Rider going with.*

*Rider leaning away.*

**Faults Commonly Occurring in Half-Pass**

- Irregular Steps
- Lack of Bend
- Loss of Impulsion
- Not Ridden to Marker
- Quarters Leading
- Quarters Trailing
- Wrong Bend

# Renvers and Travers

At the travers the horse is slightly bent round the rider's inside leg. The horse's outside legs pass and cross in front of the inside legs. The horse is looking in the direction in which he is moving. Travers is performed along the wall, or, preferably on the centre line, at an angle of about 30 degrees to the direction in which the horse is travelling. Renvers is the inverse movement to travers, with the tail instead of the head to the wall. Otherwise the same principles and conditions are applicable.

*Rules for Good Renvers and Travers*

- The renvers and travers should be ridden equally on both reins.

**Faults Commonly Occurring in Renvers and Travers**

- Angle Varied
- Lack of Bend
- Loss of Impulsion
- Resistance
- Too Much Angle

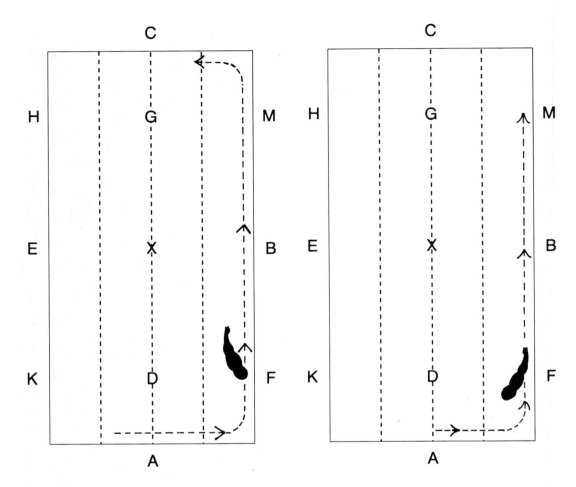

*Renvers.*          *Travers.*

- These movements should not be ridden at an angle of more than 30 degrees from the wall.
- The impulsion and forward momentum must be maintained throughout the movement.
- The rider should keep his weight very slightly over the inside stirrup, not let it slip to the outside.
- The horse must have enough bend

to look at the marker towards which he is travelling.

## Counter Change of Hand

The counter change of hand, or change from one half-pass to another, can be performed at walk, trot, canter or *passage*. At the canter, the horse is required to do a flying change between each half-pass.

*The horse in renvers; rider looking down.*

*Rules for Good Counter Changes of Hand*

- The first half-pass must be 'completed', before the new half-pass is asked for.
- The new half-pass must not be started before the horse has been straightened and the new bend taken.
- Counter changes should not be attempted in canter until the flying changes are established.
- When counting the steps of a canter zig-zag, the flying change is the first stride of the new half-pass.
- The counter changes should be practised equally on both reins.

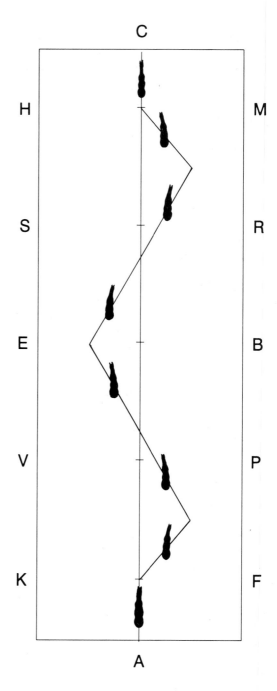

C

H        M

S        R

E        B

V        P

K        F

A

*Zig-zag.*

---

**Faults Commonly Occurring in Counter Change of Hand**

- Change not Forwards
- Quarters Leading at Start
- Resistance

---

# Faults

## *Loss of Angle*

*In shoulder-in*

The horse must remain at the same angle to the wall throughout the shoulder-in movement. The rider must remain consistent with the aids throughout the exercise and the horse must stay receptive to them.

In the early stages of training the horse should not be asked to maintain the shoulder-in position for too long; as his strength and collection improves the movement may be held for longer.

The angle of the shoulder-in is most often lost because the outside rein is not effective enough to control the outside shoulder of the horse. It would probably be better to ride the shoulder-in for a while with less bend until the shoulder is under control, and then gradually increase the bend making sure that there is no loss of angle.

## Too Little Angle

*In shoulder-in*

To ride the shoulder-in with too little angle will cause fewer problems than riding it with too much angle, as the former will not stop the horse from going forwards, which the latter would. However, too little angle will not produce the effect of collecting and engaging the horse as the shoulder-in should.

Make sure that you are asking for enough angle and that your aids are clear. If the angle is still not improved, the horse must be made to be more responsive to the aids, and the schooling whip may need to be used to back up the leg aids.

## Too Much Angle

*In shoulder-in*

If the horse is asked to perform the shoulder-in on too great an angle, it will be difficult for him to keep going forwards enough, which will probably cause him to show resistance. There is no value in increasing the angle to a greater degree as it will not help to improve the engagement or collection; in fact, it will probably do the opposite.

*In renvers or travers*

There is no benefit in riding the renvers or the travers with more angle than the 30 degrees asked for in fact this will cause difficulty and therefore resistance from the horse.

Think about riding more forwards, demanding less angle with your outside leg.

## Angle Varied

*In shoulder-in*

If the angle of the shoulder-in is varied, the rider is either not being consistent with the aids or the horse is choosing to ignore them.

Keep the aids on consistently throughout the movement: the horse must remain responsive to them. If the horse is ignoring the aids, investigate the possible cause: that he does not fully understand what is being asked of him, perhaps, or that he simply doesn't 'like' this exercise, in which case encourage and praise with the voice during practice sessions.

The angle of the travers or renvers should be maintained throughout the movement. Any deviation shows that the horse has not been truly kept between the rider's hands and legs.

Make sure that you keep the aids in place for the duration of the movement and that the horse continues to listen to them.

## Lack of Bend

*In half-pass*

As long as the horse is bent correctly in the half-pass a small lack of bend is not a great fault.

You will need to concentrate on the preparation for the movement. The horse should be correctly and sufficiently bent round your inside leg on a circle; he should then proceed out of the circle with a few steps of shoulder-in. If the horse is answering the bending aids, he may then be asked for a few steps of half-pass. If the bend begins to fail, you should return to shoulder-in position to reinstate the bend and then ask for half-pass again. In trying to improve the bend you must not lose the forward flow of the movement.

*In renvers and travers*

In both renvers and travers the horse is required to look in the direction in which he is travelling, so a lack of bend will render him unable to do this.

You will probably need to return to work at the shoulder-in to establish a better bend through the horse. Once the horse is able to show a true bend round your inside leg in the shoulder-in, work on the travers and renvers may be resumed. You must prepare the horse before the start of the movement, making sure that he has a good bend. If the bend begins to fail circle away, re-establish the bend and then resume the renvers or travers.

## Loss of Bend

*In shoulder-in*

If the horse becomes straight during the shoulder-in, the object of the exercise is lost. The rider's inside leg, on the girth, should keep the horse bent with the help of the outside leg behind the girth.

Start the shoulder-in from a circle, making sure that the horse is truly bent round your inside leg. If the bend begins to fail, immediately ride on to another circle and re-establish the bend before beginning the shoulder-in again. A schooling whip may be used to increase attention and back up the use of your inside leg.

*Travers with slightly too much bend in the neck. The rider should be on her left seat-bone with her legs more 'round the horse'.*

## Too Much Bend

*In leg-yielding*

It is a requirement of the leg-yielding exercise that the horse remains straight except for a slight bend at the poll. The rider who asks for too much bend, or the horse that of his own accord bends too much will not be able to go forwards correctly and the rider will not have the correct control over the horse's outside shoulder.

Ask for just a few steps at a time and, if the horse starts to bend too much, straighten the horse with the outside rein and send him forwards before resuming the exercise.

## Wrong Bend

*In half-pass*
If the horse takes a wrong bend position in the half-pass he is not performing the movement asked for.

*A left half-pass with the wrong bend. The rider is looking down and the left leg is not in position.*

You will need to go back a stage or two with the horse's training and teach the horse to bend correctly round your inside leg. The shoulder-in should be practised to improve and establish the bend and to gain more obedience to the aids. The half-pass should be practised from a shoulder-in position and, if the bend fails, the horse put back into the shoulder-in position again. Gradually you should be able to hold the correct position further across the arena before having to take the shoulder-in position.

## Change Not Forwards

*In counter change of hand*
This comment would apply to a counter change of hand at canter where the horse is required to show a flying change between two half-passes.

The change should be forwards and straight and is counted as the first step of the new half-pass.

When the change is not forwards, it is usually because the rider has cramped the horse in an effort to fit the movement in to the arena. The last step of the first half-pass needs to be ridden more forwards and less sideways.

## Falling onto Outside Shoulder

*In leg-yielding*
If the horse falls onto the outside shoulder during the leg-yielding exercise, it indicates that the rider has not maintained control with his outside rein. Because of this the horse will probably have too much bend in the neck as well.

Practise being able to take a slight flexion at the poll while working on a straight line. Once this has been achieved the leg-yielding exercises may be started again. If, at any point during the exercise, you lose control over the shoulder, ride forwards, straighten the horse, and then start the exercise again.

## Loss of Impulsion

### In leg-yielding
Loss of impulsion during the leg-yielding exercise usually occurs because the rider is more concerned with going 'sideways' than 'forwards', thus making the angle of the movement too steep.

Make sure that the gait is active and forwards before commencing the leg-yielding exercise. Start by riding just a few steps of leg-yielding and then ride actively forwards; then a few more steps of the leg-yield and then forwards again. In this way it should be possible to keep the impulsion and activity for longer periods.

### In shoulder-in
If the impulsion is lost during the shoulder-in the horse will not place his inside hind leg far enough under his body and the collecting and suppling object of the exercise will be lost. If the horse finishes the shoulder-in on a worse trot than he began the exercise with, the shoulder-in has been ridden incorrectly; he should in fact end on a better trot, resulting from the increased engagement of the inside hind leg.

If at any time during the shoulder-in the impulsion starts to fail, take the horse on to a circle, regain the impulsion, and begin the shoulder-in again.

### In half-pass
A loss of impulsion during the half-pass indicates that either the rider has not used his inside leg sufficiently to create and maintain the energy, or the horse has not responded to the aids given. Quite often it is the fault of the rider, being too concerned with going sideways and not enough with going forwards.

To improve the situation, practise riding less steep half-passes, sending the horse forwards from the inside leg. Use the schooling whip if need be to back up these leg aids.

### In renvers and travers
The horse should maintain the same degree of impulsion and engagement throughout the renvers or travers.

If impulsion is lost, begin work on a circle, making sure that the horse is working with impulsion and activity and then proceed to the renvers or travers, making sure that you use the inside leg to effect during the movement to maintain the energy from the horse's hindquarters. If the impulsion does begin to fail, ride the horse on to a circle, regain the impulsion, and then restart the exercise.

## Irregular Steps

### In half-pass
This fault frequently occurs in the half-pass. The horse's gait must remain regular throughout; any form of irregularity is a serious fault. Most irregularity is caused by the horse's falling onto his inside shoulder or by a lack of impulsion and engagement from the inside hind leg.

As soon as any irregularity is felt, ride the horse briskly forwards on to a circle, gaining control over the bend, engagement and suppleness of the horse. Once this has been achieved the half-pass can be recommenced, but only for a few steps at a time and not at a very steep angle. Gradually the angle and duration of the half-pass may be increased as long as no irregularity is evident.

## Too Much Neck Bend

*In shoulder-in*
This fault often occurs in shoulder-in, when the rider asks for too much bend in the horse's neck, making it difficult to keep control over the inside shoulder of the horse. In consequence, the bend is not uniform throughout the horse's length, which is what is required of this movement.

Too much neck bend is often coupled with too little angle, the horse remaining virtually straight in the track with just the neck bent round. Return to work on a circle, confirming the use and control of the outside rein. When you feel able to stay in control of the amount of neck bend, the shoulder-in may be attempted again. The amount of bend in the neck should be no more than would be seen on a 10-metre circle.

## Not Ridden to Marker

*In half-pass*
If the half-pass does not finish at the correct marker, either the rider has been careless or the horse has not answered the aids sufficiently. In competition many marks are lost through sloppy riding of the movements.

If the horse has ignored your aids he will need to be made more responsive, possibly by using the schooling whip in conjunction with the legs.

## Quarters Leading

*In leg-yielding*
If the horse leads with his hindquarters

during the leg-yielding exercise, his forward movement will be restricted.

Do not allow the horse to anticipate the exercise and move the hindquarters over before the forehand has been correctly positioned. If the hindquarters do begin to lead, ride the horse energetically forwards, then restart the exercise.

*In half-pass*
If the hindquarters are allowed to lead in the half-pass, the forward movement of the exercise will be lost. Most often this fault is seen at the start of the half-pass, either because the horse has anticipated the movement or because the rider has not prepared sufficiently.

Always prepare for the half-pass by taking the horse into a slight shoulder-in position. If at any time during the half-pass the quarters start to lead, it is better to ride forwards on to a circle, reposition the horse, and begin again.

## Quarters Leading at Start

*In counter change of hand*
The rider must be sure to complete the first half-pass parallel to the long side of the arena, ride forwards for a stride, position the forehand, and then ask for the new half-pass.

When first teaching the counter change of hand, do not be in a rush to start the second half-pass. Take two, three, or even four, strides to position the horse correctly, and then ask him to begin the half-pass. As time goes on the number of strides may be decreased.

## Quarters Out

*In shoulder-in*
If the horse's hindquarters swing out

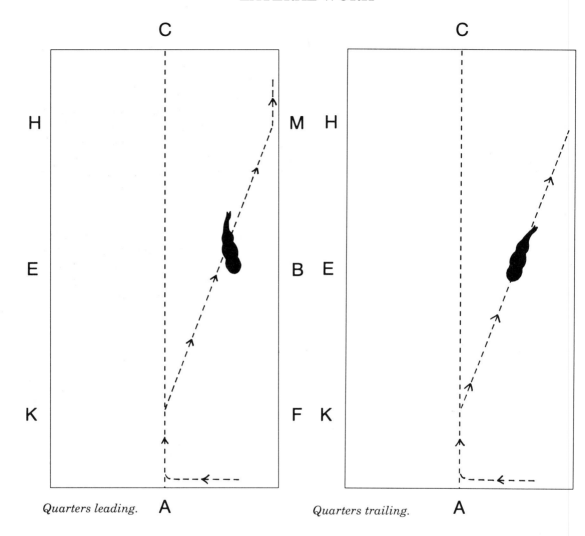

*Quarters leading.*

*Quarters trailing.*

during the shoulder-in, the whole point of the exercise has been lost: the horse is in effect putting himself in a leg-yielding position.

Great care must be taken at the start of the shoulder-in to bring the forehand off the track and not push the hindquarters out. This fault is often caused by asking for too much bend or angle or because the rider does not have his outside leg in place behind the girth.

## Quarters Trailing

*In leg-yielding*
If the horse's hindquarters appear to be trailing in the leg-yielding exercise, it is usually in fact that the forehand is 'running away'. If the forehand of the horse is positioned and controlled correctly the hindquarters should not trail.

*In half-pass*
Quarters trailing is less of a fault than quarters leading, but all the same it needs to be corrected.

You will need to make the horse more responsive to your outside leg aids and ensure that the forehand is correctly positioned. Often it is not the hindquarters that are trailing but the forehand that is running away, so ensure that the horse is answering all hand and leg signals correctly.

## Resistance

*In renvers and travers*
Resistance during any school movement should be investigated to discover whether it is caused by physical discomfort or weakness, or simply a lack of willingness to accept the aids.

By the time the horse has progressed to performing renvers and travers he should be accepting the rider's hand, seat and leg aids. If he is not, you will need to go back a stage or two and work on the easier school movements until acceptance has been achieved.

*In counter change of hand*
Resistance to the rider's aids at counter change of hand indicates that the horse is not ready to perform the movement. You must go back a stage or two to gain acceptance of the hand, seat and leg aids.

# CHAPTER 8

# Rein Back

The rein back is an equilateral, retrograde movement in which the horse's feet are raised and set down almost simultaneously by diagonal pairs. The feet should be well raised and the horse should remain straight. The horse should move forwards to the required gait, without halting, from a light signal from the rider.

When asking for the rein back, the rider's aids should be even. The legs ask the horse to step forward but the hands then restrain this response. If the horse is obedient to the aids he will step backwards. The rider must never pull; nor should the movement be asked for if the horse is overbent, hollow, or has his hindquarters disengaged.

## Faults

### Anticipation

The rein back must be executed from a square, on-the-bit halt. The horse must not move back until the rider applies the aids.

If the horse anticipates the movement he must be immediately sent forwards, the halt re-established, and allowed to back only when asked. When teaching the rein back to the horse it is important to practise a lot of halts without reining back so that the horse does not begin to anticipate the movement. However, do not take the legs away from the horse in halt to stop him reining back, as this will lead to other difficulties.

### Dragging Back

A horse that drags his feet in the rein back usually has his head too high and his back hollow. From this position he will find it very difficult to pick his feet up as required.

Make sure that the horse is on the bit at the halt, and then ask the horse to move back a step at a time. Any loss of roundness should be countered by riding forwards, re-establishing the halt, and then asking for the rein back again. The horse that drags his feet back may be helped if you assume a slightly forward seat, as this will encourage him to round his back.

### Halt Not Established

Before the rider asks the horse to move back a good halt must be established. The horse should stand square, on the bit, and attentive to the rider's aids. After the last step of the rein back the horse should move immediately forwards without halting.

If the horse anticipates the rein back, send him forwards, re-establish the halt and immobility, and then ask for the steps back.

*A correct rein-back.*

*Horse being pulled back.*

## Hollow

Hollowness in the rein back indicates that the horse has come off the bit, which means that he will not be able to pick his feet up correctly.

Ensure that the horse is on the bit at the halt, before asking him to step back. As soon as the horse tries to hollow his back, send him forwards, re-establish the halt, and begin the rein back again. Taking the weight a little out of the saddle may encourage the horse to maintain a rounder outline.

## Not Straight

The horse must remain straight throughout the rein back. Any deviation from the straight line is a serious fault and must be corrected.

Make sure that the halt is straight, square, and on the bit, before the start of the rein back. Both hands and legs must be used equally. If the horse continuously steps to one side, you may, as a correction, bend the horse a little to the direction that the hindquarters are stepping to help block them. Once the quarters are under control, you must regain the straightness.

## Rearing

Some horses – especially those that have been punished by use of the rein back – may rear in order to evade the movement.

Avoid the movement for a while, establishing the horse's obedience to the aids and his confidence in you. You may find it a help to rein the horse back in hand, so that he understands the movement.

## Resistance

Resistance to the rider's aids is a bad fault in all movements.

Use clear, concise and consistent aids at all times. It is important to teach the horse to respond to the aids at all the gaits, and at the halt, before asking for the rein back. Also, you will need to ensure that you are not using too strong a hand to ask for the rein back, thus causing the resistance.

## Running Back

At the rein back the horse must stay 'between the rider's hands and legs', in the same way as if he were moving forwards.

Any tendency to rush back must be countered by sending the horse forwards, re-establishing the halt, and then beginning the movement again. You should ask for just one or two steps at a time, and make sure that these are under control before asking for more steps.

## Slow to Move Forwards

The last hind leg to move back should be the first to step forwards. This should be achieved without a halt being established.

If the horse is slow to react to the aids, it may be necessary to use the schooling whip to back up the leg aids.

## Steps Short

The steps of the rein back should be long and well defined.

If the horse takes short steps back he must be encouraged to make them longer. The rounder the horse's outline the more likely he will be able to take a longer step. Make sure that the horse is on the bit at the halt before asking for the rein back. The horse must be asked to step back slowly and deliberately, remaining in a round outline. If the horse rushes back he is more likely to take short steps.

## Too Many Steps Back

The rider must be in control of the number of steps that the horse takes back. The horse must not be allowed to come off the aids and make his own decision.

If this becomes a problem, practise riding just one or two steps back until control has been gained.

## Wide Behind

Horses that rein back wide behind do so to avoid bending the joints of the hindlegs.

The horse should be asked to rein back for only one or two steps, and then asked to walk forwards. The rider should then re-establish the halt and repeat the exercise. Some horses find it easier if the rider takes the weight a little forwards in the saddle during the rein back. This can help to keep the horse's back round and decrease the problem of going wide behind. Once the horse has learnt to bend the hind joints correctly, the rider can resume sitting in the saddle.

---

### Rules for a Good Rein Back

- A good rein back can be achieved only from a balanced, square halt, with the horse attentive to the aids.
- The reins must never be used to pull the horse back.
- Both hands and both legs must be used with equal pressure to achieve a straight rein back.

---

# CHAPTER 9

# Piroutte

The pirouette (or half-pirouette), is a circle (half-circle), executed on two tracks with a radius equal to the length of the horse, the forehand moving round the hindquarters. Pirouettes (or half-pirouettes), may be executed at walk, canter and *piaffe*.

The forefeet and the outside hind foot move round the inside hind foot, which forms the pivot, and should return to the same spot or slightly in front of it each time it leaves the ground. At whatever gait the pirouette is executed, the horse should be slightly bent to the direction towards which he is turning, remain on the bit, turn smoothly round, and maintain the exact cadence and rhythm of footfalls of that gait. The poll should remain the highest point during the entire movement.

Pirouettes require a high degree of collection to be executed correctly. To perform the pirouette, the rider will need to collect the gait and, with a slightly open inside rein, lead the horse into the turn. The outside rein is against the horse's neck to control the amount of bend and the impulsion, and to move the forehand of the horse round the hindquarters. The rider's inside leg is on the girth to maintain the impulsion, and the outside leg is placed behind the girth to control the hindquarters.

*A walk pirouette to the right.*

## Faults

### *Changes Behind*

*In canter*
A horse that changes leg behind during the canter pirouette is avoiding placing sufficient weight onto his inside hind leg.

The rider should practise canter collecting exercises to strengthen and supple the horse more so that he is able to place the necessary weight on the hindquarters, and thus perform a good pirouette. Ensure that you keep your outside leg in place behind the girth to control the hindquarters, keep your weight a little over the inside stirrup, and do not bend the horse too much to the direction of the turn. Do not attempt to ride a full pirouette until the horse is able to maintain the correct balance and collection at the half-pirouette.

## Hollowing

### In walk

The horse must remain round and on the bit throughout all the school exercises and the pirouette is no exception.

Ensure that you have a good collected walk before attempting the pirouette, because if the horse hollows in the collected walk there is no hope of the pirouette's being correct. When the walk is correct, begin the turn, but at any sign of hollowing send the horse forwards, re-establish the collected walk, and then begin again.

## Lost Bend

### In walk and canter

The horse must maintain the bend to the direction he is turning throughout the pirouette. Loss of bend is most often seen in the last step or two of the turn, when the horse anticipates the new direction.

Practise riding out of the turn, maintaining the bend for a few steps and not letting the horse choose when to straighten. Bend is often lost because the rider uses insufficient inside leg to maintain it. You must also ensure that you keep your weight on the inside stirrup, as any deviation of weight to the outside may cause the bend to be lost.

If the bend is being lost during the turn at canter, it indicates that either the horse is not remaining sufficiently on the aids or the rider is not keeping them in place. The pirouette should be started from a very slight shoulder-fore position where the horse will be correctly bent round the rider's inside leg. If at any moment during the turn the bend starts to fail, ride the horse forwards, re-establish the bend, and then begin the turn again. As with the walk pirouette, sometimes the bend is only lost in the last stride of the turn, in which case you need to practise riding out of the turn in the shoulder-fore position.

## Not Enough Steps Round

### In canter

In a canter pirouette the horse will ideally take three or four steps for a half-turn and six or eight steps for a full turn. The horse that 'swings round' on fewer steps than this is losing the collection of the canter and escaping from between the rider's hands and legs.

The rider needs to gain control over the collection of the canter. A good exercise to stop the horse from swinging round is to ride a 'square' shape, riding a quarter of a pirouette on each corner until control has been gained over the steps.

## Not Straight Before Turn

### In collected canter

Although the horse should be bent a little to the leading leg in the collected canter, and may be taken into a slight shoulder-fore position in preparation for the turn, he should not be presented in a travers or renvers position for the turn. This exercise is sometimes used in training to help stop the horse from swinging his quarters out but must not be shown in the competition arena.

## Overturning

*In walk, canter and piaffe*

A pirouette that has 'overturned' has not finished on the same line as it started on; in fact the horse will have made a one and a quarter turn. In effect, the rider has lost control over the horse, who is turning of his own accord.

Too many riders practise only the half- or full pirouette, and the horse ends up doing them as a 'trick', rather than as a highly developed gymnastic exercise. Practise riding a different number of steps each time and riding forwards out of the turn when you want to. This will enable you to gain complete control over the strides.

## Pivoting

*In walk*

A horse that pivots in the walk pirouette has stopped going forwards and has not picked up the inside hind leg sufficiently.

To correct the problem you will need to use more inside leg to keep the activity and make the turn a little wider. Once the horse can be kept active, the turn can be made smaller again.

## Quarters Out

*In walk and canter*

If the hindquarters swing out during the pirouette the horse has ignored the outside leg aids of the rider, or the rider has restricted the forward momentum of the walk, possibly by taking too much inside bend.

Position the horse in a slight shoulder-fore position before the turn. If, during the turn, the hindquarters begin to swing, ride the horse forwards, regain control, and begin the turn again. Do not attempt to make the turn too tight too early in the horse's training, as this may cause this problem to arise.

If the horse swings the hindquarters out during the canter pirouette, he is avoiding placing sufficient weight onto his inside hind leg.

Return to the canter collecting exercises to strengthen the horse's hindquarters and to gain control over them. The horse will need to be made more responsive to your outside leg aids. Make the pirouettes larger for a while, and make sure that they are not taking too much bend in the neck, as this may also cause the quarters to go out. Once control over the hindquarters has been regained, the turn may be ridden smaller again.

## Rearing Round

*In canter*

If a horse rears round in the pirouette, he has lost the correct tempo and activity of the canter.

You need to practise collecting the canter, maintaining a greater activity of the hindquarters with not too much slowing of the tempo. Once this has been achieved you can try the pirouette again. Only one or two steps at a time should be ridden and if the tempo slows too much the horse should be ridden forwards, the correct collection regained, and the turn attempted again.

## Stepping Back

*In walk*

Although the walk pirouette is performed

*Canter pirouette to the right.*

almost on the spot, the movement must always be forwards, never back.

If the horse steps back during the turn, you must use more inside leg to keep him forward and the turn should be made a little bigger to encourage the forward movement. This problem may also arise if the rider is too strong with the hand in an attempt to make the pirouette small. Although a good contact must be maintained throughout the turn, the rider's arm must be elastic.

## Stuck

*In walk, canter and piaffe*
The expression 'stuck' means that the horse's hind feet have not kept marching throughout the turn. He must pick up each foot at every stride, not pivot on them.

To cure the problem, you must use more inside leg on the girth to create more activity and make the turn a little bigger. Once the activity has been regained, you may make the turn smaller again.

## Too Big

*In canter*
Although making large turns may be useful during schooling, a pirouette that is too big will obviously not score high marks in the dressage arena. However it is an easier fault to correct than many others. You must be careful that when you close up the turn you keep the activity of the hindquarters so that the horse does not pivot on the hind legs. In canters you will need to improve the collection and make the horse more responsive to the aids so that the turn can be ridden more in place. In the early stages of pirouette work, the horse should not be asked to make the turn too small until his hindquarters are sufficiently developed. The quality and true rhythm of the canter must not be lost in an attempt to show more collection and a tighter turn.

## Too Many Steps Round

*In canter*
In the ideal canter pirouette, the horse will take six to eight steps to complete the turn (half the number for a half-pirouette). If the horse takes more steps than this the rider is not asking the forehand to turn sufficiently with each stride.

You will need to use the outside rein a little more firmly against the horse's neck, keep the weight on the inside stirrup, and encourage him to take a longer step round.

### Rules for a Good Walk Pirouette

- A good pirouette can only be made from an active walk with the horse attentive to the aids.
- The bend must be maintained throughout the turn.
- It is better to ride a slightly large pirouette with the hind legs remaining active, than to make the turn too small and risk stepping back or pivoting.

### Rules for a Good Canter Pirouette

- The pirouette should be ridden from a slight shoulder-fore position, not from travers or renvers.
- The bend, collection and purity of the gait must be maintained throughout the turn.
- The rider must keep his weight a little more on the inside stirrup and never sit 'away' from the movement.

# CHAPTER 10

# Flying Changes

The flying change of leg (change of leg in the air) is executed in close connection with the suspension that follows each stride of canter. Flying changes of leg can be executed in series (tempi changes), for instance at every fourth, third, second or at every stride. The horse should be calm, straight, impulsive, light, and in balance. The degree of the collection may be slightly less than otherwise at the collected canter. The horse, while remaining on the bit, should show 'expression' in the change, but no resistance to the rider's aids. The series changes should not be practised until the single change is established. The aids for a flying change are the same as those given to ask the horse to strike off into canter from walk.

## Faults

### Kicking at Aid

Most horses that kick at the rider's aid in flying changes do so because the aid was given in a rough manner.

You will need to return to practising the strike-off from walk to make the horse obedient and submissive to the aids. If the aid has been correctly applied, and the horse still kicks to it, he should be brought immediately to walk, made to strike off, and the change repeated until he accepts the rider's legs.

## Late Behind

If the horse changes late behind, he has not completed the flying change while in the air. In a true change, the fore and hind legs on the same side come forwards together, but in the late change the foreleg comes forward and the hind leg follows, either within the stride (often termed 'not through'), or a stride later.

Most problems in flying changes are caused by poor canters and bad preparation. The horse must be active, forward, straight and attentive to the rider's aids to achieve a good change. The horse should be positioned for the change by the rider's taking a slight flexion towards the new leading leg, placing the outside leg behind the girth and the inside one on the girth. If the horse persists in not bringing the hind leg through, you may need to use the schooling whip in conjunction with the leg aids to help get the correct response.

## Late to Rider's Aid

The rider should always give clear, precise and consistent aids for all movements.

If the horse answers the aid to change leg a stride or more after the aid has been given, you will need first of all to make sure that the aid is clear to the horse. If the aid given is clear, but the horse still does not answer, the schooling whip may need to be used to back up the leg aids to

*Executing a flying change. The rider is slipping to the right, collapsing the back and losing her leg position.*

make the horse more attentive to them. This problem must be cleared up before a series of changes is asked for or they will never be able to be ridden accurately.

## Not Straight

Although the horse must have a slight bend to the leading leg in canter, his hind feet must follow in the same tracks as the forefeet.

Most loss of straightness seen in flying changes is caused by the rider tipping the upper body towards the change, or by too strong a use of the outside leg in the change without sufficient use of the inside

leg to send the horse forward. In the early days of flying change work, the rider's weight may be used to encourage the horse to change leg, but once he has understood the exercise you must sit still in the saddle and not throw your weight to the side. If the outside leg is used too strongly, the horse will 'half-pass' away from it, causing a loss of straightness.

## One Mistake/Mistakes

These are terms used in connection with series of changes where the correct number of steps between the changes has not been shown. These mistakes result either from rider error or from the fact that the horse has not answered the aids correctly.

Before attempting series changes, ensure that the single change to each direction is well established, otherwise the horse will become upset and confused and many problems may arise from this. If you are quite sure that the aids given are clear and understood by the horse, it may be necessary to use the schooling whip to make the horse more attentive to them.

## Quarters Swinging

A flying change or series of changes should always be straight, the hind feet following in the tracks of the forefeet.

If the hindquarters are swinging in the changes, you need to use a lighter outside leg aid and ride the horse more forwards from the inside leg.

This problem is often caused by the rider not remaining still and upright in the saddle. The weight should be kept central in the saddle during the change and not shifted to each new direction. If the habit of swinging the quarters becomes established it can be a very difficult fault to correct.

## Tension

Many horses get tense and worried about performing flying changes and the rider must be very careful not to let this become an established problem. Time must be taken to gain the horse's confidence by working on the strike-off from walk and single changes. Never attempt series changes until the horse is completely happy about performing a single change in each direction.

---

### Rules for Good Flying Changes

- Do not start to teach the flying changes until the horse is obedient to the strike-off aids from trot and walk.
- Good changes can only come about from a well-collected, calm, straight, balanced canter.
- Do not ride 'tempi' changes until the single changes to each direction are established.
- Get somebody to watch your changes from the ground to ensure that the horse is not going 'late behind', as once established this can be difficult to cure.
- Do not swing your weight to the side in the change as this will make the horse crooked.
- Always practise a little counter-canter after changes to ensure the horse is still obedient to the aids.

# CHAPTER 11

# *Piaffe* and *Passage*

## *Piaffe*

The *piaffe* is a highly measured, collected, cadenced, elevated trot appearing to remain 'on the spot'. The horse's back is supple, the hindquarters are lowered, the hocks active and well engaged. The forehand is light and mobile, the neck well arched; the poll is the highest point. The horse should remain light, on the bit, and ready to move forward at the lightest aid from the rider. He should be straight; each diagonal pair of feet is raised and returned to the ground alternately, with an even cadence and slightly prolonged suspension. In principle the height of the toe on the raised foreleg should be level with the middle of the cannon bone of the other foreleg. The toe of the raised hind leg should reach just above the fetlock on the other hind leg. The *piaffe* shows the ultimate collection of the horse at trot.

## Faults

### *Advancing*

Although the horse should appear to be trotting on the spot, the activity and impulsion of the *piaffe* will take the horse very slightly forwards.

In the early stages of training the *piaffe* the horse is best kept forward, gaining ground, as this will help to keep the hind legs active and the steps round. As the horse becomes stronger and more able to maintain his balance and collection, you should be able to half-halt and decrease the steps until they are almost on the spot. You must always retain the ability to ride the *piaffe* steps forward; the horse should never stay on the spot of his own accord.

## *Croup High*

If the croup is high in the *piaffe* the horse is not performing the movement required. In the *piaffe* the horse should take his weight onto the hindquarters, lower the croup, bend the joints of the hind legs and be light and mobile in the forehand. If the croup is high none of these criteria will have been met.

You will need to rethink your training programme and go back a few stages to teach the horse to answer the half-halt collecting aids correctly. If you are satisfied that the horse truly collects in walk and trot, you may begin the *piaffe* exercises again. Only a few steps should be asked for at a time before riding briskly forwards. If the horse accepts the lowering of the croup and the engaging of the hindquarters, more steps may be gradually asked for.

## *Earthbound*

A *piaffe* that is 'earthbound' is not

showing either the correct height to the steps or the required suspension. This is caused by a lack of activity, collection and impulsion.

To improve the height of the steps you will need to ride the *piaffe* more forwards with greater activity from the hindquarters. The collected trot should also be worked on to improve the strength in the the horse's hindquarters and to achieve more bending of the hind leg joints. Ask for a few steps at a time to begin with; as the horse gains strength more steps may be asked for.

## Irregular Steps

The steps of the *piaffe* must be regular and cadenced. Any irregularity is regarded as a serious fault. The *piaffe* should always be practised equally on both reins and the horse made to remain straight. If the horse is not straight, or is resisting the aids, irregularity will occur.

If this habit is allowed to become established it can be very difficult to cure at a later date. If resistance is the problem, establish the reason for this. Do not ask the horse to perform too many steps in the early days as great strain may be put on the hindquarters, causing the horse to be irregular.

## On the Forehand

A horse that is on the forehand in the *piaffe* is not meeting the requirements of the movement and will earn very poor marks in the arena. The whole object of the *piaffe* is that the horse lowers his croup, bends the joints of the hind legs, and shows great energy from the hindquarters. By doing this the horse is able to be light and mobile in the shoulders. If the horse is on the forehand the shoulders will not be light or mobile.

Decide whether the problem is in the *piaffe* alone or whether the horse is on the forehand in walk, trot and canter. If all the gaits are on the forehand, you should forget the *piaffe* for a while and work on using more effective seat and leg aids, combined with half-halts to engage the horse and lighten the forehand. If it is only in the *piaffe* that the problem arises, you will need to concentrate on the balance of the horse while asking for the *piaffe* steps. Only a few steps should be asked for at a time until the horse's hindquarters are strong enough to lift the forehand. If the horse begins to lose balance and tip onto the forehand the rider should ride him briskly forward in trot and then start the movement again.

## Quarters Swinging

If the horse's hindquarters swing from side to side in the *piaffe* he is avoiding taking the weight correctly on his hind legs.

You will need to make the *piaffe* more forward, ensuring that the quarters stay under control. If the quarters begin to swing, ride briskly forward, re-collect the horse, and begin the movement again.

## Snatching Hind Leg

Horses are often seen snatching one or both hind legs during the *piaffe*. This is usually caused by the trainer on the ground 'tapping' at the hind legs with a whip. Although help from the ground can be very valuable, the whip – if it is used – should be used on the croup, not on the hind legs. The rider must not rely on the trainer on the ground to produce the

*An active* piaffe, *although the poll is a little low.*

*piaffe* steps or he will find that in the competition arena he will not get any!

## Stepping Back

Although the *piaffe* appears to be performed on the spot, it should still be an active, forward movement. At no time during the movement should the horse step back or show any inclination to do so.

To cure such a problem, you will need to make the *piaffe* steps more forwards by more effective use of the legs. Once control has been gained, the *piaffe* can be brought nearer to 'on the spot', but the forward inclination must not be lost.

### Piaffe Pirouettes

Although this movement is not required in any B.H.S. or F.E.I. tests it is often shown in Grand Prix Freestyle classes. If correctly executed it is a very impressive movement earning high marks, but unfortunately it is rarely shown in this way and should not be attempted until the piaffe is well established and completely under the rider's control.

To perform a piaffe pirouette, begin the piaffe steps on a straight line. If the steps are active and correct, you may use the walk-pirouette aids to ask the horse to start the turn. The horse's hindquarters must be kept under control and not allowed to swing out (as is so often seen), so that the movement ends up as a turn on the centre instead of a pirouette. Only a few steps should be asked for in the beginning until the horse is able to maintain a good piaffe for a full pirouette. The turns should be practised equally in both directions.

## Passage

The *passage* is a measured, highly collected, very elevated, cadenced trot. Each diagonal pair of legs is raised and returned to the ground alternately, with cadence and prolonged suspension. The neck is raised and arched; the poll is the highest point. In principle the height of the toe of the raised foreleg should be level with the middle of the cannon bone on the other foreleg. The toe of the raised hind leg should be slightly above the fetlock joint of the other hind leg. The *passage* should always be a joy to watch.

## Faults

## *Hollowing*

At all times during the *passage* the horse should remain on the bit and round. Any sign of hollowing should be corrected at once so that it does not become an established habit.

Some trainers misguidedly allow the horse to hollow in order to raise the forelegs more, but this is wrong; even if the forelegs do come higher, the hollowness restricts the hind legs, which are then not able to step under the horse correctly, thus causing the movement to be broken.

Extra height in the steps should come from increased activity of the hindquarters, not by artificially raising the head.

## *Irregular*

The steps of the *passage* should be regular, cadenced and free from any tension or irregularity. Irregularity may be caused by the horse being crooked or by a lack of strength in one hind leg. The *passage* should never be practised for long periods as it puts a great strain on the horse's hindquarters.

If the horse does not have a physical problem, and riding him straight does not bring the lazy leg through, you may need to put the horse in a slight shoulder-in position to encourage engagement of the lazy leg. Once the activity and regularity has been achieved the horse must be straightened again.

## *Lacking Height*

If the *passage* steps lack height it indicates that more activity and engagement from the horse's hindquarters are needed.

The steps should never be raised by use of the hand alone as this will only make the horse hollow. Higher steps can be developed by riding the horse from medium trot to *passage*, using the impulsion from the medium trot to lift the *passage*. If the steps start to fail, repeat the exercise.

## Nose Behind Vertical

In all the collected work, the front of the horse's head should be just in front of the vertical.

Often, in an effort to achieve the *passage*, the rider overuses the rein aids rather than increases use of the seat and leg aids to achieve height in the steps. If the horse is overbending, rather than just bringing the nose a little behind the vertical, then this is a far more serious fault as it indicates that the horse has dropped the rider's contact. In this case, the horse must be ridden strongly forwards each time he drops the contact, and the movement resumed when the correct contact has been gained.

## Not Clear or Not Direct

This is a comment used by judges when the transitions from the *passage* to the *piaffe*, and vice versa, are not obvious.

In the early stages of putting the two movements together, the *piaffe* should be ridden forwards to maintain the engagement and make it easier for the horse to proceed in the *passage*. As the horse becomes stronger in the hindquarters he should be able to make a direct transition from one movement to the other. The transitions should be direct, clear, straight, and show no resistance to the rider's aids.

## Reluctance

This is seen in the horse that begins the *passage* without sufficient acceptance of the rider's aids.

This fault is often seen after the *piaffe*, when the horse is reluctant to go forwards to the *passage*. The fault here lies in the *piaffe*: the horse has not remained active enough from the rider's legs and resents being asked to go forward. The *piaffe* should be practised more forwards until control over the impulsion is gained and you are able to ride forward when you wish.

---

**Rules for Good Piaffe and Passage**

- Teach the horse piaffe before beginning passage.
- Never practise too many steps at one time until the horse's quarters are strong enough.
- Practise piaffe and passage equally on both reins.
- In piaffe, keep the horse 'thinking forwards'.
- Make sure that you always have the ability to ride the piaffe forwards; never allow the horse to come behind the bridle and stay in place of his own accord.
- Have someone watch from the ground so that any irregularities can be picked up and corrected at an early stage.
- Do not allow the trainer on the ground to create the steps for you as you cannot take him into the arena with you!
- Do not attempt to swing your weight from side to side to make the steps higher, as the horse may start to cross his legs, which can be a very difficult fault to correct once established.

---

# CHAPTER 12

# Test Riding

There is much more to entering a show than just training the horse to perform the movements required in the test. The rider must decide how many tests to enter and learn them. He must bring his horse to the required level of training and have him fit enough to cope with the extra demands on him, such as travelling etc.

A young horse will need to be shown white boards, white lines, tubs of flowers, and so on. He should also be prepared for the sound of cameras, loud-speakers and crowds. He will probably not be used to trotting directly at a car or judge's box so this must also be practised.

Many dressage horses are trained at home in very quiet surroundings without other horses being present. The rider will need to introduce him to working with others so that he does not become too excited on the day. Some riders have special tack, or clothes kept especially for a show. These should be worn a few times beforehand so that neither rider nor horse is unsettled by them.

## Number of Tests to Ride

Many novice riders make the mistake of entering their horse in too many classes at a competition. A horse that is tired will never give his best. It is better to ride one or two tests well than to perform four or more moderate ones!

Most people ride their horses each day at home for only forty-five to sixty minutes, yet they expect the horse to perform for up to three hours at a show! The initial 'riding in' will probably last for about thirty minutes, the test eight to ten minutes. As you can see, forty of your sixty minutes have already been used up! Further tests should require less preparation but if there is a long gap between them this may still add half an hour for each extra test you ride.

## Learning Tests

Learning tests comes easily to some people but is more difficult for others. Personally I have always found that the easiest way was to draw the test out on a piece of paper and keep going over it until I had learnt it.

Each individual will have to find his own way to cope with this, but a word of warning: DO NOT practise the test too often on the horse you are going to compete on or he will begin to anticipate the movements.

## Freestyle Tests

Freestyle tests are now ridden at all levels of dressage from Novice to Grand Prix.

The rider must first study the 'sheet', to

be aware of all the compulsory movements to be ridden. Movements above the standard of the test **must not** be shown. For example, Shoulder-In must not be included in a novice freestyle test.

In an attempt to make the test interesting riders often try to include too much, which, from the judge's point of view, just looks muddled. Try to make the test symmetrical, repeating the exercises on both reins in a balanced way.

During practice sessions at home, time the test. This is of great importance, but bear in mind that a test timed on a grass arena may vary quite a lot if the competition arena is deep sand! The time begins at the first salute and ends at the final salute.

## Turnout

It is only fair to your horse, the judge and yourself that you make an effort to appear in the arena looking smart and tidy. Too often riders say, 'I didn't bother to plait as this show is not a qualifier!' This is a poor attitude to adopt. If you can't be bothered to turn out properly, why should the judge bother either!

## Riding In

Riding in is probably the hardest thing for a competitor to get right. Every horse will react differently under show conditions, as will every rider. Young horses take longer to settle but will also tire more quickly. Older horses can take some time through stiffness.

When loosening the horse up, aim to follow the same pattern as you do every day at home. The sense of familiarity this

---

### Riding to Music

Riding to music can be great fun but it involves a lot of preparation. The aim is to find music that fits the individual horse's gaits. It is rarely possible to use other people's music as this involves having to alter the horse's stride to fit the music. This should never be done: the music should always be made to match the horse's stride.

Setting a metronome to each of the horse's gaits enables the rider to select suitable music in the comfort of his home. Once several pieces have been selected they should be tried to see which appear to enhance the gaits rather than detract from them. However, the rider will need to bear in mind that on different surfaces the horse will move in a slightly different tempo.

Only practice will show how to fit the music and the movements together. Some people put the music together first: two minutes' trot, one minute's walk, two minutes' canter; and then design a test round it. Others make up the test first and then fit the music to it.

No movements that are above the standard to which you are competing are allowed to be included, so, in a medium-standard freestyle test, flying changes must not be shown.

---

brings will help to keep both of you calm.

Preparation for a test should include a loosening period followed by a warm-up exercise to put the horse on the aids and to gain his concentration. It is not a time for 'teaching' him; this should have been done at home!

Only by trial and error will you be able to establish the optimum riding-in time; and even then this will not be rigid as, in different circumstances and as the years go by, the time needed will change!

# Riding the Test

## *Entering the Arena*

Many marks are lost because the rider enters the arena badly.

Some arenas are not well placed so a sharp turn onto the centre line cannot be avoided, but if this is not the case the rider should give the horse plenty of room to enter from a straight line.

Although the judge must not be kept waiting, do not be rushed into the arena if you are too near 'A' when the hooter is sounded. It is better to go round the arena once more and enter in a calm manner.

Decide at home which way you are going to ride around the arena. Is your horse straighter on the right or the left rein? Which rein does he halt the best from?

As a rider I always preferred to enter the arena on the same rein as the turn at 'C'.

## *Tension*

Riders often complain that their horse rides in well but then gets tense in the arena.

I hate to have to say it but I believe that most of the tension comes from the rider. The only tension that may come from the horse is if he is seeing sights for the first time that might worry him, such as flowers in tubs, and so on. If this is the case more preparation should be done at home. (*See* Spooking.) Once the horse has learnt to be tense in the arena, he will remember past experiences and retain the habit, even if his rider remains calm. Do all you can to prepare yourself and your horse for competition.

Give your horse as much confidence as you can in the arena: a pat on the neck, or use of the voice may lose a mark or two, but it will bring many rewards in future tests.

---

**Camera Shyness**

A person bending down by the arena or the noise from a camera shutter going off can severely upset some horses.

The only way to make the horse confident and attentive to you is to work him at home with people stationed around the arena clicking their cameras until the horse is no longer bothered by them. Avoiding the situation will make matters worse not better!

---

## *Accuracy*

At the lower levels, accuracy should never be placed above the correct way of going, but as the standard of the tests becomes higher the rider should be able to show both.

The correct riding of the figures should be shown at all levels. Many marks are thrown away by novice competitors riding circles of the wrong size and inaccurate-sized loops.

## *Anticipation*

Anticipation of the movements by the horse is very commonly seen in the arena and may come about for several reasons.

The most usual reason is that the rider has practised the test too often at home and the horse knows what is coming next. The answer is obviously not to practise the test: the movements may of course be practised but not always in the same order as they appear in the test.

Horses 'tune in' to their riders and because the rider is – by necessity – thinking of the next movement, the horse reads these signals and acts upon them before the rider asks. This may be difficult to correct but, with good preparation, and by teaching the horse to listen to the aids, it can be put right given time.

The most often seen 'anticipation' occurs after the walk. As the rider begins to take up the reins the horse anticipates a transition to trot or canter. The rider must, at home, remember to practise taking up the reins after a walk and either drop them again, or ride a circle in walk, before proceeding into trot or canter. In this way the horse will not anticipate when the reins are picked up.

## Spooking

If the horse 'spooks' in the arena it is because the rider has not sufficiently prepared him at home, and he is not enough between the hand and leg.

During the horse's training, introduce him to such things as white boards, tubs of flowers, and any similar things that you are likely to encounter so that he is not frightened by them at a show.

Also check that the horse is correctly attentive to the aids. The horse must not be able to escape from between the hands and legs. If this is happening, you must work on the acceptance of the aids to be able to keep control of the horse.

## Leaving the Arena

It is stated in the rule book that after the final halt, the rider should proceed towards 'C' on the centre line, turn left or right, and from 'M' or 'H' take a straight line to 'A'. Many variations on this theme are shown by riders and, although most judges are too busy giving the 'end marks' to comment, the correct route should be ridden.

# Self-Assessment and Improvement

## Learning from the Judge's Sheets

It always surprises me as a judge and trainer how many riders fail to read the remarks made on the sheet by the dressage judge. Some riders do not even bother to collect their sheets! I am not saying that every judge gets it right every time but even the most novice judge usually has a point to make.

The whole idea of riding a dressage test is to have your progress checked. We all get into bad habits riding on our own at home and faults like lacking bend in one particular direction, or your leaning to one side will be noted by the judge and should be taken on board by the rider.

## Learning from Watching

Watching other riders – good or bad – performing dressage tests is probably the best way to learn what to do and what not to do! Unfortunately many riders are too wrapped up in their own riding to use this excellent way of learning.

If it is possible to watch from 'C', behind the judge, you will get the best view to learn from. Failing this, 'A' is the next best place. Watching from the side line is interesting but not so revealing.

## Watching Yourself

One of the best training aids to come on to the market must be the video camera. You can learn so much about your performance from watching yourself on film.

If possible, the filming should be done from behind the judge at 'C' or from 'A' so that your view is the same as the judge's.

## Showing Too Often

With the number of shows being held today, many riders are tempted to compete too often. Not many years ago, there was no winter season; and this was a time to train the horse for the next level. Nowadays it is possible to compete every week throughout the year.

Young horses competed too often will become stale and overtired, not just through the competitions themselves but through the travelling, preparation and attendant stress and excitement that inevitably goes with it. Older horses will be bored and lack the necessary sparkle.

Showing too often will also restrict the horse's progress. Too often I hear my pupils say, 'I can't practise rein-back, flying changes, *piaffe*, and so on, because I have a show this weekend!' Competing at a show should be a 'check' on the horse's progress, not an end in itself.

**Rules for Good Test Riding**

- Arrive at the show in good time.
- Know your tests well.
- Always collect your sheet and read it.
- Do not ride too many tests on one day.
- Do not practise the tests too often or the horse will anticipate the movements.
- Always be riding a stage higher at home than you are competing at.
- Have yourself and your horse well turned out.
- Remember there is always another day!

# CHAPTER 13

# Dressage Terminology

**Aids**   The aids are the means by which the rider conveys his wishes to the horse. The natural aids are the seat, the back, the weight, the hands and the legs (use of the voice is not permitted in the dressage arena); the artificial aids are the whip and spurs. The rider must learn the aids for the different movements and apply them correctly and consistently. Aids given should never be rough or inconsistent and should be barely visible from the ground.

**Above the Bit**   A horse is said to be 'above the bit' when the head is carried too high and the back is hollow. This is a serious fault as the horse cannot work correctly in this outline and the muscles will develop in the wrong way. The rider must teach the horse to accept the hand and leg aids and work him towards a rounder outline. (*See* 'On the Bit'.)

**Balance**   The horse carries his weight on all four legs: by nature the forelegs bear the greatest weight as they have to carry the head and neck. The rider also throws additional weight on to the forehand, making matters even more difficult for the horse. The art of dressage riding is to balance the centre of gravity of the horse and rider so that more weight is placed on the hindquarters, giving the forehand more freedom and lightness. This is achieved when the horse lowers his croup, bending the joints of the hind legs more and placing the hind feet further under the body. This will be possible only if the horse is straight and accepts the aids correctly.

The rider will feel whether his horse is balanced by the ease with which he performs the movements. If his work feels laboured, or he trips or slides or throws his head around, he will certainly be lacking in balance.

Seen from the ground he will appear heavy in his forehand having a lot of his weight on his shoulders. His hindquarters will be out behind him with the hind legs being used behind the buttocks instead of where they should be, under the body.

**Broke**   A term used to describe the fact that the horse has interrupted the required gait with another. It is most often used when the horse is in walk and jogs for a few steps.

**Contact**   Contact is the 'feel' that the rider has on the horse's mouth through the reins. The horse should at all times accept this feel and the rider should make sure that it is consistent and elastic. This will be possible only if the rider has an independent seat and the horse has been taught to accept the aids.

The rider should first of all make sure that the horse is going forwards from the leg. Only if the leg aids are answered will the horse be submissive in his mouth. The submission is felt by a yielding to pressure of the bit. This is achieved by a feel and ease action of the fingers, which should provide the elastic contact that the rider is seeking.

**Counter-Canter**  A movement in which the horse is asked to canter on the opposite lead to the direction in which he is travelling. In walk, trot or true canter the bend is towards the direction in which the horse is travelling; in counter-canter the bend is held to the leading leg.

The counter-canter may feel awkward to the rider at first and a good way to develop the feel is to ride shallow loops approximately 3 metres in from the track on the long side of the school. In this way both rider and horse can develop the balance needed for the exercise to be a success. Any breaking into trot or difficulty may mean that the aids have been incorrect or have failed. Make sure that the correct aids for canter to the appropriate leg are maintained through the loop.

**Cadence**  A horse is said to have cadence when, through engagement and impulsion, rhythm and acceptance, the horse is able to maintain a tempo that shows energy and elegance.

**Diagonal  (Rider)**  Riding on the 'correct diagonal' means that in rising trot the rider should sit in the saddle as the inside hind leg and outside foreleg are on the ground. This helps the horse to become equally supple to both sides. One school of thought says that it should be the other way round so that the rider is out of the saddle as the inside hind leg comes forwards, thus enabling more freedom for it to step further under the body.

Conventional wisdom dictates that by sitting as the inside hind leg is coming forward it will encourage it to come further under. Whichever way you adopt the most important thing is that you change the diagonal each time you change direction so that the horse does not become stiff on one diagonal.

**Disunited**  If a horse is 'disunited' it means that he is not cantering with the legs in true sequence. In effect he is cantering in one direction with the front legs and to the other direction with the hind legs. This fault most often occurs through stiffness: the horse is avoiding bringing his inside hind leg under his body. The rider must make sure that his outside aids are in place and that the horse is listening to them. Small circles or tight turns should not be attempted until the horse is more supple and strong enough to take his weight onto his inside hind leg. If he does disunite he should be asked to trot and the canter restarted.

**Error of Course**  If during a dressage test the rider takes the wrong course the judge will ring the bell and ask the competitor to start again from where the error occurred.

**Half-Halt**  The half-halt is a checking and rebalancing aid used to 'call the horse to attention' to prepare him for the next movement. It can be used to shorten the steps, improve the contact, and to gain collection and engagement. The rider should sit deeper in the saddle, close the legs and 'check' with the outside rein. This may be very slight or quite firm if necessary. As the half-halt is a balancing aid the rider must remember to ride forward after it in balance, not on the forehand.

The feel of a correct half-halt is of the horse being gathered together and the steps being active and springy. When seen from the ground the half-halt is rather like a momentary pause but without any loss of momentum or rhythm.

**Hollowing**   Hollowing can happen at all gaits and is the result of the horse's not accepting the rider's aids correctly, especially the bit. He will be working with his head too high causing his back to be 'hollow' rather than 'round'. From the ground, the topline of the horse will appear dipped in the middle. The rider will need to take a firmer contact with the horse's mouth and use more effective leg and seat aids to send the horse forwards into the bridle. A horse continually ridden in a hollow outline will develop his back and neck muscles incorrectly and will become very difficult to correct.

**Impulsion**   Impulsion is the controlled energy that propels the horse forward from engaged hindquarters, balance and acceptance of the aids.

The rider will feel the impulsion when the horse is actively going forwards, and his back is supple and soft to sit on; the horse should never pull or lean on the rider's hands. When watching a horse full of impulsion he will contain life and presence and be purposeful in his going.

***Losgelassen***   A German word meaning 'loose and supple'.

***Losgelassenheit***   A German term meaning 'A horse that freely gives all its muscles to use its whole body without any resistance'; the horse is supple and unconstrained.

**On the Bit**   A horse is said to be on the bit when the hocks are correctly placed, the neck is more or less raised and arched according to the stage of training and the extension or collection of the gait, and he accepts the bridle with a light and soft contact and submissiveness throughout. The head should remain in a steady position, as a rule slightly in front of the vertical, with a supple poll as the highest point of the neck; no resistance should be offered to the rider.

Having first used his legs the rider will feel a yield to his hands when pressure is applied on the bit and in appearance the horse should represent an arc over his topline.

**Open Rein**   The inside rein when taken away from, and to the side of, the horse's neck. The open rein is used to 'lead' a young horse through a turn or onto a circle, and may be used to ensure that the horse is answering the rider's inside leg.

**Outline**   The 'shape' that the horse forms from his poll to his croup. It should be 'rounded', never hollow. This is important because only in this outline can muscles develop in the right way.

**Overtracking**   When the hind feet come to the ground in front of the prints left by the front feet.

**Pacing**   A horse is said to 'pace' when instead of maintaining a four-beat rhythm in walk, he walks laterally, with the legs on the same side coming forwards at the same time. A horse may also 'pace' in trot: he brings the legs on one side forwards together instead of working them in diagonal pairs.

**Pivoting** A term used to describe a horse's failure to keep walking with the hind legs during a walk pirouette.

**Port** A port is an indentation of greater or less depth in the centre of the mouth-piece of a Weymouth bit, giving the horse sufficient room for his tongue.

**Rhythm** The regularity of the horse's steps and the correctness of the beats of the gait.

**Riding In** Warming up in preparation for a horse's daily work or for a competition. The rider should form a routine way of working the horse in to settle and relax him and to prepare him physically and mentally for the work to follow.

**Schwung** A German term which means that the horse is working 'through'; the power generated in trot and canter, conducted forward through the swinging, rounded back of the horse.

**Shoulder-Fore** The shoulder-fore position is used to straighten the horse in canter and to prepare for strike-offs, pirouettes, and so on.

The rider uses the same aids as for the shoulder-in but does not bring the forehand so far over. Sometimes it will just be brought in line with the hind-quarters; sometimes a little more to the inside.

**Stuck** A term used to describe the failure of a horse to pick up the hind feet at each stride during a walk pirouette.

**Tempi Changes** Tempi, or sequence, changes are a required movement in advanced tests, the horse being asked to

perform flying changes at every fourth, third, second or single stride.

**Tilting** Carrying the head at an angle instead of straight. The rider will notice that one ear is carried lower than the other. This fault occurs when the horse is not accepting the bit evenly on both sides of the mouth and sometimes because the inside hind leg is not active enough. The rider needs to work to gain the correct acceptance of the bit and also to make sure that his contact is even. Most riders are stronger in one hand, so great care needs to be taken to ensure that the horse is not given more pressure on one side of the mouth than the other. The legs must also be used equally to ensure that the horse works correctly from behind and is straight.

**Track Left or Right** To track left or right the rider will change direction through 90 degrees by riding a quarter of a small circle (as at a corner), and finish on the outer track.

**Transitions** Transitions are changes either from one gait to another or within a gait (collected to extended walk, for example). In the arena they should be shown as the rider's knee passes the marker. The horse should remain straight, in balance, and on the bit, showing no resistance to the rider's aids.

**Turn Left or Right** For a simple turn left or right the rider will change direction through 90 degrees by riding a quarter of a small circle (as at a corner), beginning before reaching the marker and finishing on a line at right angles to the track and directly opposite the marker.

On all turns the rider should feel that

his horse is curved to the degree of the turn. Also he must make sure that the turn does not in any way cause the horse to be unbalanced or to alter the rhythm of the steps.

***Uberstreichen*** A German term that means 'stroking the horse's neck'.

**Working in** *See* 'Riding In'.

**Wrong Lead/Leg** A horse is said to be on the wrong leg or wrong lead during canter if his leading leg is on the side opposite to the way he is bent and the direction in which he is travelling.

**Zig-Zag** Zig-zag is a term used to describe a series of half-passes connected by counter changes of hand.

# Index